"I can think of few things that the contemporary church needs to recover as much as the ancient practice of lectio divina. In my view it is the primary mode by which we are to receive Scripture. The focus of this series is rightly on the biblical text itself, and the commentary and questions push us back to the text to listen for God's address. My hope is that this well-written and accessible tool will assist readers in the practice of lectio divina."

—**Craig Bartholomew**, coauthor, *The Drama of Scripture*

"Stephen Binz has done an admirable job of introducing his readers to the process of lectio divina and immersing them in it. Through teaching the practice of this ancient way of studying the Bible, this series of Scripture studies will recharge and deepen the faith and lives of many, who thereafter will use the art for private devotions and/or in small groups. I heartily recommend this series to individuals and churches who want to join in the spirited revival of Christianity in our time!"

—**Marva J. Dawn**, Regent College

"At their recent Synod the world's Catholic bishops recommended lectio divina to all Christ's disciples, for prayerfully reading and making God's Word one's spiritual nourishment follows well-trod paths in the Christian tradition. Stephen Binz guides us on these paths in his Ancient-Future Bible Study series. I am pleased to recommend this project with enthusiasm."

—**Terrence Prendergast, SJ**, Archbishop of Ottawa

"Lectio divina, despite its centuries-long use, is still little known outside of monastic and academic settings. Ancient-Future Bible Study, a project that does great credit to Brazos Press, has in mind to correct that historical defect in Christian piety."

—**Patrick Henry Reardon**, author, *Creation and the Patriarchal Histories*

"Ancient-Future Bible Study brings a centuries-old approach to Scripture and prayer into the twenty-first century, providing sound commentary, thoughtful insights, and meaningful suggestions for personal reflection and meditation. Stephen Binz invites us to open our minds and hearts to the transforming power of God's Word. Under his guidance, the wisdom of the Bible comes vividly to life."

—**Carl McColman**, author, *The Big Book of Christian Mysticism*

"Stephen Binz has a knack for popularizing the Bible. His latest series, Ancient-Future Bible Study, demonstrates once more his ability to give people sound guidance as they read the Bible. I am happy to warmly recommend this modern application of the ancient method of lectio divina—the once and future way to read the Bible prayerfully—centered on fascinating characters from the Old and New Testaments."

—**Fr. Ronald D. Witherup**, author, *The Bible Companion*

"A method of Bible study that has a long and celebrated history in the church is given renewed momentum with this series. The goal here is more than instruction. The five movements of lectio divina are an invitation to immerse oneself in the riches of our biblical tradition and to give flesh to that tradition in our daily lives. This series will be a wonderful aid for the development of one's spiritual life."

—**Dianne Bergant, CSA**, Catholic Theological Union

"This series is a wonderful gift for the church in late modernity. In an era of twittered attention, we have inculcated all sorts of bad reading habits that we then bring to Scripture. The Ancient-Future Bible Study prescribes a counter-formative regimen: the personal and communal practice of lectio divina or 'sacred reading.' For some this will be a strange, new practice; but it will quickly feel as natural as breathing. So find some friends, take up this series, and read anew!"

—**James K. A. Smith**, Calvin College; author, *Desiring the Kingdom:
|Worship, Worldview, and Cultural Formation*

"Stephen Binz's new series allows us to put down the commentaries and word studies and let the beautiful poignancy of the text seep into our souls, all with the aid of the Holy Spirit. I heartily recommend it."

—**Tony Jones**, Solomon's Porch, Minneapolis; author,
The New Christians: Dispatches from the Emergent Frontier

"Stephen Binz, a responsible biblical scholar and experienced pastor, has undertaken the important project of leading non-professional but committed readers of the Bible into a spiritually enlivening encounter with the biblical text through engagement with some of the fascinating characters who people its pages. Anyone yearning to pray the biblical text will find this series a useful companion."

—**Sandra M. Schneiders**, Jesuit School of Theology

ΛΝCIENT-FUTURE BIBLE STUDY

PAUL

Apostle to All the Nations

STEPHEN J. BINZ

BrazosPress

a division of Baker Publishing Group
Grand Rapids, Michigan

© 2011 by Stephen J. Binz

Published by Brazos Press
a division of Baker Publishing Group
P.O. Box 6287, Grand Rapids, MI 49516-6287
www.brazospress.com

Printed in the United States of America

Library of Congress Cataloging-in-Publication Data
Binz, Stephen J., 1955–
    Paul : apostle to all the nations / Stephen J. Binz.
        p.   cm. — (Ancient-future Bible study)
    ISBN 978-1-58743-278-1 (pbk.)
    1. Paul, the Apostle, Saint—Textbooks. 2. Bible. N.T.—Textbooks. I. Title. II. Series.
BS2507.B56 2011
225.9′2—dc22   2010021408

Scripture is taken from the New Revised Standard Version of the Bible, copyright © 1989, by the Division of Christian Education of the National Council of the Churches of Christ in the United States of America. Used by permission. All rights reserved.

Some content from "Welcome to Ancient-Future Bible Study" originally appeared in Stephen J. Binz, *Conversing with God in Scripture: A Contemporary Approach to Lectio Divina* (Ijamsville, MD: The Word Among Us Press, 2008).

11   12   13   14   15   16   17   7   6   5   4   3   2   1

Contents

Acknowledgments

For the past several years my work has focused on making connections between ancient practices and contemporary experiences. My speaking, writing, and counseling under the umbrella of Bridge-Building Opportunities has emphasized the link between past and present, East and West, time-honored tradition and progressive renewal in the fields of biblical theology, Christian spirituality, and personal growth.

When I discovered the mission of Brazos Press, I felt that I had found a new home. By its own definition, Brazos Press is "staked on the discernment that while various existing Christian categories (liberal and conservative, mainline and evangelical, even Catholic and Protestant) prove increasingly unserviceable, there is at the same time occurring a robust renewal of classical, orthodox Christianity across many of the old lines or borders." This is a publisher that is eager to cross boundaries, build bridges, and extend the vital roots of the ancient Christian tradition into the twenty-first century.

I am grateful to Jim Kinney, associate publisher and editorial director of Baker Academic and Brazos Press, for supporting my work. Lisa Ann Cockrel, editor for this series, has masterfully guided these books through the editorial process and improved this work with her many ideas. I also appreciate the skillful work of Lisa Beth Anderson, Rodney Clapp, Steve Ayers, BJ Heyboer, Jeremy Wells, Caitlin Mackenzie, and the whole Brazos team for their efforts to refine and promote this project.

The term "Ancient-Future" seems to perfectly express the bridge between ancient wisdom and future possibilities that I want to create in this series. The term is applied in a number of other spheres to emphasize a blending of tradition and innovation. In the arts, ancient-future music and dance is created through fusing centuries-old traditions with contemporary genres and technology. By learning from the world's great traditions and ancient practices, artists create cross-cultural expressions that are richly profound yet also widely appealing.

I am particularly indebted to the work of the late Robert Webber, many of whose titles use the term "Ancient-Future" to express his mission of drawing wisdom from the past and translating those insights into the present and future life of the church, its faith, worship, ministry, and spirituality. In his own words: "My argument is that the era of the early church (AD 100–500), and particularly the second century, contains insights which evangelicals need to recover." This series resonates with his outstanding work and hopefully, in some small way, will honor his memory and continue his vision.

Finally, I am grateful to all my friends and colleagues in the field of biblical studies and to all pastors, lay ministers, and church volunteers who are dedicated to an anciently rooted and forward-looking Christianity. Particularly I want to express my appreciation to my wife Pamela, a professor of music, for the loving support and inspiration she constantly offers to me.

Welcome to Ancient-Future Bible Study

Ancient-Future Bible Study unites contemporary study of the Bible with an experience of the church's most ancient way of reading Scripture, *lectio divina*. By combining the old and the new in a fertile synthesis, this study helps modern people encounter the *sacra pagina*, the inspired text, as God intends it for the church. Through solid historical and literary study and the time-honored practice of lectio divina, the mind and the heart are brought into an experience of God through a careful and prayerful reading of the biblical texts.

As the Word of its divine author, the Bible is not just a literary anthology of ancient texts; it is inspired literature addressed to God's people. God intends the sacred texts to move from our heads to the depths of our hearts and to form us as a new people living in God's reign. Ancient-Future Bible Study guides readers to listen to Scripture within the tradition and scholarship of the church in order to unleash its life-changing potential.

The ancient art of lectio divina is rooted in the Jewish tradition of Jesus, and it was nourished through the desert spirituality of the early centuries, the patristic writers of the ancient church, and the monastic tradition through the ages. In our day, lectio divina is experiencing a worldwide revival as Christians are returning to age-old wisdom to experience the Scriptures in a deeper and more complete way.

As you experience Ancient-Future Bible Study, you will realize how the church's long tradition of biblical study, reflection, prayer, discernment, and contemplative action can enrich your discipleship. You will learn how to dispose yourself to be formed by the Word of God as you join with the array of men and women through the ages whose lives have been transformed by that same living Word.

Reasons for Studying the Bible

Most often people study the Bible for one of three reasons. First, they study for information and knowledge. This usually includes a search for historical facts, doctrinal truths, and moral guidance. Second, they study to find advice for solving a personal need or getting through a life crisis. This usually involves seeking out lists of specific passages that speak to the particular needs of the moment. Third, they study so they can defend their faith and witness to others. This usually consists of choosing selected passages to remember and quote, so they can argue for a particular approach to faith or help lead others toward the truth. While all of these objectives can lead to good results, their accomplishments are always limited and partial.

The most complete reason for studying Scripture is for the purpose of encountering the living God through the sacred text. This divine encounter leads not just to more information and advice but to a deeply rooted transformation of life. The inspired Word evokes a spiritual transformation within the lives of those who allow God's Word to do its true work, urging us to personal growth in Christ and fuller discipleship.

For Scripture to have its deepest effects in us we must approach the text with humility, reverence, and expectation. As we receive its revelation and understand its truth, Scripture has the ability to gradually change our minds and mold our hearts. Unlike any other literature, the words of the Bible can renew our lives when we approach the text as an encounter with its divine author.

The Indwelling of the Holy Spirit

The Bible was written under the inspiration of the Holy Spirit. God's "breathing in," acting in union with the human authors of the texts, makes the Scriptures the Word of the living God. Because God is the primary author of the Bible, we can be assured that the texts have a power that transcends that of any other spiritual reading.

God's inspiration of the biblical books does not refer only to a past reality, to the historical time in which the biblical authors were guided to write the texts. Rather, the work of God's Spirit is an ongoing reality within the inspired books. The sacred texts remain inspired; they are forever permeated with divine breath and are filled now with the Spirit of God.

This understanding of the Spirit's enduring and ongoing presence in the biblical texts is the foundation of lectio divina. Through the Holy Spirit, God addresses his Word to us here and now through the ancient text. Because of the indwelling Spirit, the Word is alive and has the power to transform us. The Word of God is charged with creative power to change and renew us from within.

The Movements of Lectio Divina

Lectio divina (LEK-tsee-oh dih-VEEN-ah) is best translated, though incompletely, as "sacred reading." Its revitalization, like the renewal of other spiritual practices from the early church, is becoming a means of deep spiritual growth for people today. Lectio divina helps us return to the most ancient understanding of the sacredness of the inspired text. The Bible is not like a textbook, used for looking up factual documentation, nor is it like a manual, describing a how-to method for solving problems. Rather, it is a means of forming our life in God and joining us to the story of God's people.

The process of lectio divina appeals not only to our minds but also to our imaginations and feelings. We seek to understand and experience Scripture as a real communication, as God personally addressing us. In practicing lectio divina, we get caught up in the literature and learn to love the text itself; we read it reflectively, lingering over it, and let it reach the depths of our hearts. We let go of our own agenda and expectations, gradually opening ourselves to what God wants us to experience through the sacred page.

There is no single method for the practice of lectio divina. It is not a rigid step-by-step system for encountering God in biblical passages. The spiritual masters of the early church distrusted methods of prayer and spiritual practice that were too rigidly defined, wishing instead to cultivate the freedom necessary to respond to the Spirit's promptings. Lectio divina aims toward a holistic experience of Scripture, incorporating our intellects, feelings, and actions.

Ancient-Future Bible Study incorporates five "movements." Comparable to the movements in a classical work of music, each movement has its own characteristics and can even be practiced independently of the others. There is plenty of room for personal interpretation within the tradition. Individually and together, lectio, meditatio, oratio, contemplatio, and operatio contribute to the full experience of lectio divina.

Pronunciation Guide

Lectio—LEK-tsee-oh
Meditatio—meh-dih-TAH-tsee-oh
Oratio—oh-RAH-tsee-oh
Contemplatio—con-tem-PLAH-tsee-oh
Operatio—oh-peh-RAH-tsee-oh

Lectio—*Reading the Text with a Listening Ear*

Lectio is more than ordinary reading. It might best be described as listening deeply—what St. Benedict in the sixth century described as hearing "with the ear of our heart." This listening requires that we try to receive God's Word with as little prejudgment as possible, as if we were hearing it for the first time. Lectio urges us to create a space within us for the new wisdom and understanding God wants to give us through the sacred page.

Saint Ambrose in the fourth century urged readers to avoid the tendency to read large passages in haste: "We should read not in agitation, but in calm; not hurriedly, but slowly, a few words at a time, pausing in attentive reflection. . . . Then the readers will experience their ability to enkindle the ardor of prayer." We might even consider returning to the ancient practice of reading texts aloud in order to instill within ourselves the sense of reading Scripture as a deep listening.

The essential question to ask in this first movement is, "What does the text say and what does it mean?" The Jewish rabbis and the church's patristic writers show us that there is no clear distinction between studying and praying Scripture. The more we come to understand the text with our minds, the more we are capable of being changed by the text. Wrestling with the text and seeking to comprehend its meaning is an important part of encountering God there and being changed by that encounter.

Once we've read the text slowly and carefully, Ancient-Future Bible Study invites us to learn from the commentary that follows the biblical passage. This too is part of listening to the text, only here we listen with the understanding of the church and with some basic insights of biblical scholarship. This listening to the text, with its multiple layers of meaning and rich history of interpretation, forms the foundation on which we experience the subsequent movements of lectio divina. We do what we can to make sure our reading of the text is faithful and true, so that we don't reduce God's revelation to our own imaginary constructions. On this firm basis, we construct the process of prayerfully encountering God's Word.

We might read the text as literature, looking at its words, metaphors, images, and characters. We could look at its structure and its literary form— is it poetry, parable, history, proverb, legal code, epic, or apocalypse? We should realize that God's truth is expressed in a variety of types of literature, each type expressing truth in a different way. The more we can comprehend something of the original historical, cultural, literary, and religious context of the passage, the better we will be able to probe all the potential the text can offer us.

In lectio, the words of Scripture become the means of God speaking to us. As God's Spirit guided the human authors to express the truth that God wished to entrust to the Scriptures, God also guides us through that same Spirit as we read the Bible as God's Word to us.

Meditatio—*Reflecting on the Meaning and Message of the Text*

The question to ask in this movement is, "What does the text say to me and mean to me?" Meditatio aims to bring the biblical passage into the sphere of my own life as I seek to understand how the Scripture passage speaks to me today.

Though there is a wide gap of time, language, and culture between the world of the biblical writers and our own world, meditatio bridges that gap. By reflecting on the text as well as on our own experiences, thoughts, challenges, and questions, we can grow in our understanding that God is speaking personally to us through the scriptural text. This reflection forms connections between the text of yesterday and the today of our lives.

Ancient-Future Bible Study stimulates meditatio through the use of questions for reflection. These questions encourage a deeper and more personal consideration of the text. They challenge the reader to create a dialogue between the ancient text and life today. As the Word of God, the Bible has a richness of meaning that can be discovered in every age and every culture. It has a particular message that can be received by everyone who listens to God's Word in the context of daily experiences and in the same Spirit in which it was written.

The more we meditate on God's Word, the more it seeps into our lives and saturates our thoughts and feelings. Meditatio allows the dynamic Word of God to so penetrate our lives that it truly infuses our minds and hearts and we begin to embody its truth and its goodness.

Oratio—*Praying in Response to God's Word*

Careful lectio and reflective meditatio open the way for God to enter into our hearts and inflame them with the grace of his love. There, at the core of our being, we naturally want to respond to the One whose voice we have heard. Oratio is our prayerful response to God's Word.

Lectio divina is fundamentally a dialogue with God, a gentle oscillation between listening to God and responding to him in prayer. When we recognize that God has offered us a message that is unique to our own lives—an insight, a challenge, a comfort, a call—we arrive at the moment when we must ask ourselves, "Now what am I going to say in response to God?" This is the moment of prayer.

Oratio is not just any form of prayer. It is born from the experience of listening to God in Scripture. The biblical words we have heard and reflected on become the words of our prayer. The style and vocabulary of our prayer are enriched through the inspired words of the biblical tradition. Whether our oratio is an act of praise or thanksgiving, of petition or repentance, we pray in response to what we have heard. Our prayers no longer consist of mechanically repeated formulas. Rather, they resonate with the faith, hope, and love that animated the people of the Bible in their journey with God.

Ancient-Future Bible Study offers examples of this type of prayer. After each session of lectio and meditatio, we are encouraged to continue in intimate prayer to God, melding the words, images, and sentiments of the biblical text with personal thoughts, feelings, and desires arising from the heart.

Contemplatio—*Quietly Resting in God*

Both oratio and contemplatio are forms of prayer. Oratio is our active, word-filled prayer in response to God's Word. Contemplatio is prayer without words. It is the response to God that remains after words are no longer necessary or helpful. It is simply enjoying the experience of quietly being in God's presence.

Contemplatio requires that we let go of any effort to be in charge of the process. When we feel God drawing us into a deeper awareness of his divine presence, we gradually abandon our intellectual activity and let ourselves be wooed into God's embrace. We no longer have to think or reason, listen or speak. The experience resembles that of lovers holding each other in wordless silence or of a sleeping child resting in the arms of his or her mother.

Though we may think the movement of contemplatio is passive and uneventful, it is not. When we humbly expose our heart, the center of our being, to God, what happens within us during those moments is really not up to us. In contrast to the rapid, noisy communication of our technological world, quiet, receptive stillness is the atmosphere in which the most important communication occurs. God's grace is truly at work in those moments, and the Holy Spirit is changing us without our direct knowledge or understanding.

Operatio—*Faithful Witness in Daily Life*

After reading, reflecting, and praying over a scriptural passage, we should be impacted in a way that makes a difference in our daily lives. Operatio is our lived response to the biblical text. The question operatio calls forth from us is, "How can I live out the Word of God that I have heard in my heart?"

We cannot prayerfully read Scripture without being changed in some specific way. As we deepen our relationship with God through the movements of lectio divina, our actions become vehicles of his presence to others. We become channels of God's compassion and mercy, becoming "doers of the word, and not merely hearers" (James 1:22), bringing about God's loving purposes in our daily lives.

Contemplatio and operatio should not be totally distinct and separate. Their impulses grow together in the heart of one who prayerfully reads Scripture. Contemplatio does not separate us from the world, and operatio is not genuine unless it grows out of contemplative reflection. Apart from contemplatio, operatio could become superficial pragmatism.

The Bible should never be viewed as simply a collection of maxims to be put into practice. Rarely does Scripture offer us concrete details about what to do in specific situations. Our human reason and experience must always accompany our prayerful discernment as we decide how to live out the Word of God. Listening, reflection, prayer, and contemplation are all necessary components from which flows the operatio of Christian discipleship. Lectio divina helps us become contemplative activists and active contemplatives.

The Essence of Lectio Divina

The movements of lectio divina are more like the colors of a rainbow than clearly defined stages. They overlap, blending into one another, ebbing and flowing according to the rhythm of the divine Spirit and the human heart. The five movements used in Ancient-Future Bible Study are part of a rich tradition, though additional phases are sometimes found in other historical forms of the practice: studium (study), cogitatio (reflection), consolatio (comfort), discretio (discernment), deliberatio (decision making), compassio (compassion), and actio (action).

While the most ancient practice of lectio divina is not a rigid system of biblical reflection, nor does its method require any particular steps, there are a few characteristics that identify the authentic practice of lectio divina:

✝ *Lectio divina is a personal encounter with God through Scripture.* The text itself is a gateway to God. Through the inspired Scripture, we meet the God who loves us and desires our response.

✢ *Lectio divina establishes a dialogue between the reader of Scripture and God*. The attentive reader listens to God through the text and responds to God in heartfelt prayer. The heart of lectio divina is this gentle conversation with God.

✢ *Lectio divina creates a heart-to-heart intimacy with God*. In the Bible, the heart is a person's innermost core, the place from which one's deepest longings, motivations, decisions, memories, and desires arise. The prayerful reader responds to God's Word with the whole heart and thereby grows in a relationship with God at the deepest level of intimacy.

✢ *Lectio divina leads to contemplation and action*. There is a moment in all true love that leads to a level of communication too deep for words. Prayerful reading inevitably leads to that deepest form of communication with God, which is loving silence. In addition, all true love must be expressed in action. Eventually words become inadequate, and love must be demonstrated in deeds arising from a changed heart.

The Word of God and its power to change us are gifts from God that we must accept into our lives. In order to receive the gift of divine intimacy, we must create the necessary conditions within us. Openheartedness, faithfulness, and expectation will enable us to more readily listen and receive. The more we remove the obstacles in the way—our inner resistance, our fear of intimacy, our impatient awareness of time, our desire to control the process, and our self-concern—the more we can expect Scripture to transform our lives.

Sometimes the changes are remarkable; more often they are subtle. We gradually become aware that the fruit of studying the Bible is the fruit of the Spirit: "love, joy, peace, patience, kindness, generosity, faithfulness, gentleness, and self-control" (Gal. 5:22–23). When we begin to notice this fruit in the way we live each day, we will know that the Word of God is working within us.

Your Personal Practice of Ancient-Future Bible Study

✢ This study is designed to provide maximum flexibility so that you can make lectio divina a regular part of your life according to your circumstances. If you are able to make the time in your daily schedule, you will want to reflect on one chapter each day. If not, you may select three weekdays to read three chapters per week. Or if your weekends are more leisurely, you may choose to reflect on two chapters per weekend.

‡ Reading Plan #1—30 days/5 weeks
  • Engage six lessons per week

‡ Reading Plan #2—60 days/10 weeks
  • Engage three lessons per week

‡ Reading Plan #3—90 days/15 weeks
  • Engage two lessons per weekend

‡ Whatever pace you choose for your practice of lectio divina, try to find a regular time during the day that can become a pattern for you. Choose a quiet and comfortable place where you will be undisturbed during the time of your lectio divina.

‡ During your regular time for lectio divina, try to rid yourself of as many distractions as possible. Before you begin reading the Bible, take time to call upon the Holy Spirit for guidance. Light a candle, ring a chime, kiss the Bible, or do some other action that will designate these moments as sacred time.

‡ Read the biblical text slowly and carefully. Read the passage in another translation, if you wish, to help your understanding. Don't hesitate to mark up this book with highlights, underlining, circles, or whatever will help you pay attention and remember the text and commentary.

‡ Follow the movements of lectio divina outlined in each section. Realize that this is only a tentative guide for the more important movements of God's Spirit within you. Write out your responses to the questions provided. The questions following the lectio are objective questions synthesizing your reading of the text and commentary. Those under meditatio are more personal questions, requiring thoughtful reflection. Try also to write comments on the sections of oratio, contemplatio, and operatio, according to the suggestions provided. The very act of writ-

ing will help you clarify your thoughts, bring new insights, and amplify your understanding.

‡ Approach your lectio divina with expectancy, trusting that God will indeed work deeply within you through his Word. Through this experience, know that you are placing yourself within a long procession of God's people through the ages who have allowed themselves to be transformed through lectio divina.

‡ Finally, try to be accountable to at least one other person for your regular practice of lectio divina. Tell a spouse, friend, spiritual director, or minister about your experience in order to receive their encouragement and affirmation.

Bringing Ancient-Future Bible Study to Churches

Throughout the history of salvation, God's Word has been directed first and foremost to a community, not just to individuals. The people of Israel, the community of disciples, and the early church were the recipients of God's self-communication expressed in the Scriptures. For this reason, studying the Bible in the context of a community of faith can deepen and enrich our individual experience.

Churches and other faith communities may choose to adopt Ancient-Future Bible Study and encourage its use in a variety of ways. Since this Bible study is ideally suited both for personal use by individuals and for communal practice, congregations are able to respect the many ways people desire to make Scripture a priority in their lives. By encouraging an array of options for participation, churches will increase the number of people in the congregation who are making reading and reflection on the Bible a regular part of their lives in Christ.

Collatio—The Communal Practice of Lectio Divina

The ancient term for the communal practice of lectio divina is collatio (coh-LAH-tsee-oh), a term that originally meant "a bringing together, interchange, or discussion." Its aim is building up a spiritual community around the Word of God. Collatio began in an age when books were rare and precious. Today, when everyone may have their own Bible, collatio may be practiced in many different ways.

Here are some ways of building up a faith community with Ancient-Future Bible Study:

‡ Offer this study to people who want to participate only on their own. Respect the fact that many people don't have the time or desire to gather with others. Instead they can be encouraged to read and reflect on their own with the prayerful support of the whole community.

‡ Promote the formation of informal groups made up of family, friends, neighbors, or work associates.

‡ Facilitate usage of the study through online communities or social networks. Online group members might want to commit themselves to sending an email or text message to the group offering their insights after reflecting on each Scripture passage.

‡ Set up small groups that meet regularly at church facilities or in homes. These groups may meet at different times throughout the week to offer convenient options for people in different circumstances. Groups could be made up of people with obvious connections: young adults, retired seniors, parents with young children, professionals, couples, etc. These groupings may encourage a deeper level of personal reflection among members.

Biblical reading and reflection on a regular basis is an important part of Christian discipleship. Every member of our congregations should be encouraged to make Bible reading and reflection a regular part of their lives. This is best accomplished when pastoral leadership promotes this practice and when people are personally invited to participate. When practicing lectio divina within a community of faith, we learn to place our own lives into the story of God's people throughout the ages.

Further Help for Groups

‡ Additional information for facilitating small groups with Ancient-Future Bible Study may be found starting on page 161 of this book.

✢ Since Ancient-Future Bible Study is divided into units of six lessons, motivated groups may choose to study five lessons per week on their own, with a weekly group session discussing insights from the daily lessons and practicing the sixth lesson of the week in the group.

✢ Groups with less daily time to study may divide the six lessons in half, choosing to study two lessons per week on their own, with a weekly group session discussing insights from the daily lessons and practicing the third lesson of the week in the group.

✢ The practice of lectio divina for each lesson will take about thirty minutes for an individual. Those who wish to spend extended time in reflection and prayer should allow for more time. The group session, using the suggestions at the back of this book, will take about ninety minutes.

✢ Additional information about Ancient-Future Bible Study, with descriptions of published and upcoming studies, may be found online at www.brazospress.com/ancientfuturebiblestudy. You can also connect to the series and its author on Facebook.

Introduction to *Paul:*
Apostle to All the Nations

Paul's influence on the growth and development of the Christian faith was enormous. God called Paul to bring the gospel to all the nations of the world. He was the great "apostle to the Gentiles." Paul's missionary life demonstrates how Christianity evolved from its Jewish origins into a worldwide church that embraces believers of every nationality.

Though, as a persecutor of Christian believers, Paul seemed an unlikely candidate for this work, as it turned out, he was just the right person to carry out this expansive mission entrusted to him. Paul lived in three cultures: he was a Jew, a Greek, and a Roman—possessing the ideal background for someone who would bring the message of Jesus Christ to the great cities of his day.

First and foremost, Paul was a Jew. He considered himself as belonging to God's chosen people, he was loyal to the Torah, he maintained his Jewish identity in the midst of a pagan world, and he awaited the coming of the kingdom of God, the age to come foretold by the prophets of Israel. "I myself am an Israelite, a descendant of Abraham, a member of the tribe of Benjamin" (Rom. 11:1), he proudly proclaimed. He was "circumcised on the eighth day, a member of the people of Israel, of the tribe of Benjamin, a Hebrew born of Hebrews" (Phil. 3:5). Judaism was a noteworthy religion within the empire, and grand synagogues could be found in most of the major cities throughout the Mediterranean world. Paul always remained a proud member of this ancient faith and understood his mission within the context of its sacred Scriptures.

Paul was also a Greek, and his world was that of Hellenistic culture. Since the days of Alexander the Great, Greek had been the second language and the framework of thought for everyone reached by his conquests. Because Paul was a native of Tarsus, a great center of Greek learning, he not only spoke Greek, in addition to Hebrew and Aramaic, but Greek culture, philosophy, and rhetoric enriched his mind and his viewpoint. He read the Scriptures in Greek, the Septuagint version of the Old Testament, and so was able to explain the Scriptures in the language of his audience.

Paul was also a citizen of Rome, a privilege he gained through his family and often used to his advantage throughout his missionary work. In the days of Jesus and Paul, Rome ruled the world from East to West. Paul used the massive system of Roman roads and commerce to travel thousands of miles, mostly on foot, establishing churches in cities throughout the Roman world. Yet, Paul was not an uncritical inhabitant of the empire of Caesar. The cult of emperor worship and the massive power of the empire to crush those who tried to interfere with its absolute authority were strong contrasts to the way of Christ. In the face of the imperial propaganda that proclaimed Caesar as savior and lord of the whole world, Paul's gospel message of Christ's lordship was defiantly subversive.

Paul described himself as a man who had become "all things to all people" (1 Cor. 9:22). He used his global, multicultural, and breadth of thought for the sake of the universal gospel he proclaimed. Paul was a man who could talk with rabbis on the streets of Jerusalem and with philosophers on the streets of Athens. He felt at home in the world. He knew the ancient wisdom of the Hebrew Scriptures, and he knew the wisdom of Greek literature, such as that of Homer, Sophocles, and Plato. He possessed a Jewish name, Saul, and a Greek and Roman name, Paul.

Discipleship for Paul meant proclaiming a gospel that was expressed through the Scriptures and symbols of Israel (the Torah and the temple), through the language and worldwide thought patterns of Greece (philosophy and rhetoric), using the communication and transportation systems of Rome to his advantage. He traveled up to the temple in Jerusalem for the feasts of Israel, and he journeyed along the Roman roads to all parts of the world. He knew that the God of Israel was the Creator and Sustainer of the whole world, and therefore he became a man of the whole world in order to bring the very Jewish message of the gospel to all people.

Questions to Consider

‡ What are some of the reasons God chose Paul to bring the gospel to the world?

‡ How can my understanding of the languages, cultures, and wisdom of the world help make me a better disciple?

God's Saving Plan for All the Nations

By the end of the first century, Christianity was a worldwide, predominantly Gentile religion. The transformation of a messianic movement within Judaism into the global church was in no small measure due to the mission and teachings of Paul. Yet, Paul's turn to the Gentiles was not just the result of a slow response among the Jews; rather, Paul's mission to the nations was rooted in God's ancient revelation to Israel.

God had revealed to Abraham that he would be "the ancestor of a multitude of nations" (Gen. 17:4) and that in his offspring "all the families of the earth" would be blessed (Gen. 12:3; see 22:18). The prophets and sages of Israel taught that while God sustains a special relationship with Israel, his rule extends to the entire universe. According to the Hebrew Scriptures, God's Servant would play a decisive role in bringing God's salvation to all people. God said to his Servant, "I will give you as a light to the nations, that my salvation may reach to the end of the earth" (Isa. 49:6).

As a result of Paul's experience of the risen Lord, he began to reinterpret and understand his Jewish Scriptures in the light of Christ's coming. He was convinced that Jesus died on the cross so that in him "the blessing of Abraham might come to the Gentiles" (Gal. 3:14). He saw that God's ancient desire to bring salvation to the nations was being fulfilled through Jesus, God's Servant and Messiah. Though always a Jew himself, Paul spearheaded the church's outreach to the peoples of the world, breaking down the barriers between the Jews and Gentiles.

The Acts of the apostles offers a broad sweep of Paul's incredible missionary outreach, from Jerusalem "to the ends of the earth" (Acts 1:8). Luke, the writer of Acts, places Paul on a level with Peter and the original apostles. His call to be an apostle was based not on human election but on the sheer grace of his special calling from God. Paul envisioned the church's mission field divided between Peter, sent by the Lord to the circumcised Jews, and himself, sent to the uncircumcised Gentiles (Gal. 2:7–8). In light of the church's missionary mandate to bring the gospel to the world, Luke focuses the first half of Acts on Peter and the second half (Acts 13–28) on Paul.

Questions to Consider

‡ Why is it necessary to read the Old Testament in order to understand God's complete saving plan for the world?

‡ How did Paul come to understand that God's salvation was destined to extend to all the people of the earth?

Paul's Letters and His Theology

Fortunately, Paul not only traveled and preached but also wrote letters. These letters reveal many of Paul's personal characteristics and a fair amount about his life. In them we find a man of passionate zeal and deep love for Christ and the people of his churches. Chronologically speaking, his letters were penned closer to the historical events of Christ's earthly life than any other writings in the New Testament. Because of them, Paul is rightfully called the church's first theologian.

Providentially, someone collected Paul's letters, edited, and published at least some of them. By the end of the first century, after Paul's martyrdom, his letters were being read in the churches throughout the empire, and they made an enormous impact on Christian thought.

Nowhere does Paul write a methodical exposition of his teaching. His letters are forged in the midst of travel, change, and controversy. Usually we are reading only one side of an ongoing conversation between Paul and the people in the church he addresses. Our challenge is always to consider the circumstances that gave rise to his teaching and to discerningly separate his contingent advice from his permanent doctrine.

All thirteen of the Pauline letters contain his characteristic greeting, "grace and peace to you." This is a remarkable combination of a Greek salutation, grace (*charis*), which seems to summarize the gospel in a single word, and the ancient Hebrew blessing, peace (*shalom*), which expresses the fullness of well-being that God desires for his people. In this unique greeting, Paul addresses Gentile and Jewish believers together, as members of the one church.

Notice that Paul did not write, "Charis to you Greeks and shalom to you Hebrews." Grace is not just for Gentiles and peace is not just for Jews. God desires the whole body of Christ to receive his grace and to experience his shalom. Paul wrote with respect for his readers' own ethnic and cultural backgrounds, yet he pointed to a new countercultural reality—a community in which the barriers between Jew and Gentile are broken down and eliminated.

Writing to congregations that were often divided and torn by factional strife, Paul's greeting was a concrete reminder to believers that they were called to be a "new creation." While affirming the diversity of each part of the community, Paul transcended their differences to forge a new identity. The church is not a congregation created by simply linking Jews and Gentiles together but a united body of Christ, a transformed people made new in the risen Lord.

Questions to Consider

✝ How did the writings of Paul evolve from occasional letters addressed to scattered communities to sacred Scripture for the whole church?

✝ In what way is Paul's salutation, "grace and peace to you," a characteristically Christian greeting? What does it say about the church?

Crossing Boundaries and Removing Barriers

Lectio

Read this verse, which summarizes the heart of Paul's teaching, as if he were addressing you directly. Expect these words to impact your mind and heart in a way that can transform your life.

2 CORINTHIANS 5:17

So if anyone is in Christ, there is a new creation: everything old has passed away; see, everything has become new!

Continue listening to God's Word as you also listen for the ways this Scripture passage has transformed God's church.

The heart of Paul's teaching is the experience of union with Christ. We live in Christ; Christ lives in us. We are united with Christ through faith in his saving cross and resurrection. Crucified with Christ, the old self dies, and in his resurrection, we live a new life.

This new life involves a new way of seeing, a new way of being, a new way of living—indeed a new identity. To be "in Christ" means to live as a "new creation." As a new creation "in Christ," we are incorporated into the saving community, the body of Christ. This is a community in which boundaries that divided people are broken down, in which distinctions among people no longer matter.

In Paul's day, the world was divided between Jews and Gentiles, slaves and free people, women and men. But Paul envisioned a Christian community that not only included all of these but also brought them into interdependent relationships. Part of the dramatic witness the church offered to first-century society was this attractive, alternative community of dissimilar people called into a higher unity in Christ.

Paul was a boundary breaker, always seeking to remove the barriers that divided people from one another and from God. And Paul teaches us that the church must be a boundary breaker too. Today our culture continues to be divided along lines of ethnicity, race, class, and gender. Yet, when we listen to Paul, we discover possibilities that can transcend our differences and join us into a common unity. Life in Christ is liberated life. A believer is no longer imprisoned by the prejudices, resentments, and jealousy that so often dominate human life. As Paul speaks to us, he speaks a message of "grace and peace." When we extend grace to and make peace with one another, we become boundary breakers, and, in so doing, we offer a powerful witness of Christ to our world.

Meditatio

Consider how this Scripture passage is challenging you as a member of Christ's body today.

✣ How can the church respect differences and diversity among people while seeking a higher unity?

✣ How can I become a boundary breaker and thus witness to Christ today?

Oratio

After listening with the church to God's Word, respond in prayer to God with the new understanding you have gained.

Father of our Lord Jesus Christ, you have promised to extend the blessings of your salvation to all the people of the earth. As you called Paul to proclaim your gospel to the world, you have called your church to make disciples of all the nations. Enlighten and encourage me as I read and contemplate your inspired Word in the life and letters of Paul.

Continue praying from your heart . . .

Contemplatio

Spend some moments in quiet, placing your life in the life of Christ. Trust that God is creating you anew as he works deep within you.

Operatio

How can I best dedicate myself to the reflective study of these sacred texts of Paul over the coming weeks? What regular place and time could I choose for the quiet practice of lectio divina?

1

Saul Encounters
the Risen Lord

Lectio

Light a candle, ring a chime, or perform some other gesture to sanctify this time and space for encountering God through the words of the inspired Scripture. Read this familiar passage as if for the first time, letting go of all your expectations of what you suppose it will say.

ACTS 9:1–19a

¹Meanwhile Saul, still breathing threats and murder against the disciples of the Lord, went to the high priest ²and asked him for letters to the synagogues at Damascus, so that if he found any who belonged to the Way, men or women, he might bring them bound to Jerusalem. ³Now as he was going along and approaching Damascus, suddenly a light from heaven flashed around him. ⁴He fell to the ground and heard a voice saying to him, "Saul, Saul, why do you persecute me?" ⁵He asked, "Who are you, Lord?" The reply came, "I am Jesus, whom you are persecuting. ⁶But get up and enter the city, and you will be told what you are to do." ⁷The men who were traveling with him stood speechless because they heard the voice but saw no one. ⁸Saul got up from the ground, and though his eyes

were open, he could see nothing; so they led him by the hand and brought him into Damascus. ⁹For three days he was without sight, and neither ate nor drank.

¹⁰Now there was a disciple in Damascus named Ananias. The Lord said to him in a vision, "Ananias." He answered, "Here I am, Lord." ¹¹The Lord said to him, "Get up and go to the street called Straight, and at the house of Judas look for a man of Tarsus named Saul. At this moment he is praying, ¹²and he has seen in a vision a man named Ananias come in and lay his hands on him so that he might regain his sight." ¹³But Ananias answered, "Lord, I have heard from many about this man, how much evil he has done to your saints in Jerusalem; ¹⁴and here he has authority from the chief priests to bind all who invoke your name." ¹⁵But the Lord said to him, "Go, for he is an instrument whom I have chosen to bring my name before Gentiles and kings and before the people of Israel; ¹⁶I myself will show him how much he must suffer for the sake of my name." ¹⁷So Ananias went and entered the house. He laid his hands on Saul and said, "Brother Saul, the Lord Jesus, who appeared to you on your way here, has sent me so that you may regain your sight and be filled with the Holy Spirit." ¹⁸And immediately something like scales fell from his eyes, and his sight was restored. Then he got up and was baptized, ¹⁹and after taking some food, he regained his strength.

After allowing the Scripture to penetrate your mind and heart, listen for further understanding of the text through the church's scholarship and teaching.

The scene recounts the beginning of Saul's transformation from the church's most notorious enemy to its greatest evangelist. We first encounter Saul as the leader of a violent persecution of the Jews who followed Jesus, seeking to destroy this new movement and dragging its adherents to prison. But while Saul is on his way to Damascus, his life is radically changed. Luke describes this transformation as both an external, objective manifestation of God in history as well as an intensely personal, internal conversion. The flashing light and commanding voice are reminiscent of ancient theophanies, particularly the encounters of Moses with God (Exod. 3:2–6; 19:16–20). Knowing that he is in the divine presence, Saul falls to the ground and hears the penetrating voice: "Saul, Saul, why do you persecute me?" (v. 4). In response to Saul's question, "Who are you, Lord?" the voice replies, "I am Jesus, whom you are persecuting" (v. 5).

Saul's divine encounter brings him to new, life-altering understandings. He realizes that Jesus had truly risen from death to glory, just as his disciples claimed. Saul also recognizes that the risen Jesus is identified with his followers. The church is the living body of Christ, the tangible presence of Christ in the world, a theme Saul will develop in his own letters. Saul will gradually be told what to do, but from this point on, his life is totally reoriented. No longer the proud persecutor, he is blinded and helpless, led by the hand into Damascus (v. 8).

Ananias, a disciple of Jesus in Damascus, is chosen to help bring Saul into the Christian community there (vv. 10–14). Ananias is told that not only has Saul become a believer but he is also Christ's chosen instrument "to bring my name before Gentiles and kings and before the people of Israel" (v. 15). Ironically, the one who desired to persecute those who invoke the name of Jesus will now go forth to bring that name to the world. The one who did so much evil to cause affliction for those who call on Christ's name will now be shown how much he himself must suffer for the sake of that holy name (v. 16).

The author describes the young church with a number of terms in this passage. In addition to the living presence of Christ in the world (v. 5), the church is called "the disciples of the Lord" (v. 1), "the Way" (v. 2), the "saints" (v. 13), and "all who invoke [the name of the Lord]" (v. 14; Acts 2:21). It is into this community of believers that Saul is brought. After a period of waiting in darkness, fasting, and praying, he is welcomed into the family of Christ and called "brother" (v. 17). With terms reflecting the initiation rituals of the early church, Saul receives the laying on of hands, is filled with the Holy Spirit, receives baptism, and is welcomed into the community's table fellowship. In a state of childlike dependence, Saul is escorted into the kingdom. The one who was blinded by the light will now become a light to the nations.

Meditatio

After seeking to understand the meaning of Saul's conversion for the
early Christians, ask yourself the meaning of his experience for us today.
Allow his encounter to interact with your own experiences of call and
conversion.

‡ The early Christians referred to their path as followers of Christ as a
journey—the Way. How have I experienced the path of my discipleship
as a journey under the call and leading of Jesus?

‡ Why would Jesus have selected this zealous enemy of the church as his
chosen instrument to evangelize the nations? In what way does the call
of Saul demonstrate Christ's words to his other apostles, "You did not
choose me but I chose you" (John 15:16)?

‡ Conversion experiences are often accompanied by feelings of rootlessness,
personal doubt, and confusion. Helpless and led by the hand of another,
Saul was brought into the community of disciples. Why is this time of
childlike dependence so necessary to enter the kingdom?

Oratio

Use this prayer to lead you into your own prayerful response to God's Word.

Risen Lord, you called Saul from his state of zealous certainty to a condition of helpless dependence. Give me the humility to trust in your way for my life so that I can respond to your guidance and direction. Help me to believe and follow you.

Continue to pray to God from your heart...

Contemplatio

Imagine that you are, like Saul, blind and helpless before God. Let the Holy Spirit gradually fill your heart to dispel your confusion and fear.

After a period of quiet contemplation, write a few words about your experience.

Operatio

The Word of God can change us and shape us, as it did Saul. What newness, growth, or movement have you noticed within yourself as a result of your lectio divina today?

2

Saul Boldly Proclaims
Jesus as the Messiah

Lectio

As you read the Scripture and commentary, highlight or underline passages that seem most pertinent to you. These marks will help you recall your experience of hearing the Scripture and seeking to understand its significance.

ACTS 9:19b–31

[19]For several days he was with the disciples in Damascus, [20]and immediately he began to proclaim Jesus in the synagogues, saying, "He is the Son of God." [21]All who heard him were amazed and said, "Is not this the man who made havoc in Jerusalem among those who invoked this name? And has he not come here for the purpose of bringing them bound before the chief priests?" [22]Saul became increasingly more powerful and confounded the Jews who lived in Damascus by proving that Jesus was the Messiah.

[23]After some time had passed, the Jews plotted to kill him, [24]but their plot became known to Saul. They were watching the gates day and night so that they might kill him; [25]but his disciples took him by night and let him down through an opening in the wall, lowering him in a basket.

²⁶When he had come to Jerusalem, he attempted to join the disciples; and they were all afraid of him, for they did not believe that he was a disciple. ²⁷But Barnabas took him, brought him to the apostles, and described for them how on the road he had seen the Lord, who had spoken to him, and how in Damascus he had spoken boldly in the name of Jesus. ²⁸So he went in and out among them in Jerusalem, speaking boldly in the name of the Lord. ²⁹He spoke and argued with the Hellenists; but they were attempting to kill him. ³⁰When the believers learned of it, they brought him down to Caesarea and sent him off to Tarsus. ³¹Meanwhile the church throughout Judea, Galilee, and Samaria had peace and was built up. Living in the fear of the Lord and in the comfort of the Holy Spirit, it increased in numbers.

Continue listening for the meaning of the text with the help of the church's teaching and scholarship.

Saul immediately begins his apostolic mission in Damascus, proclaiming in the synagogues, to the bewilderment of those who hear him, that Jesus is the Messiah and Son of God. Clearly he has been converted for a purpose, called to bear fruit for God's kingdom. As in his later work in the cities throughout the world, he preaches first in the synagogue and then moves to other venues to speak to the Gentiles. Though called to be an apostle to all the nations, he respects the order of God's saving plan: "to the Jew first and also to the Greek" (Rom. 1:16). The gospel that was destined for all the world is offered first through Judaism, the ancient faith of Jesus, Saul, and all the apostles.

Saul amazes his audience with his growing rhetorical power and by "proving" that Jesus is the Messiah (v. 22). The verb indicates that Saul gathered scriptural texts that show Jesus to be the long-awaited Messiah of Israel. The ongoing ministry of Paul indicates that this expert in the Hebrew Scriptures reread and interpreted all of those ancient texts in light of his experience of the risen Lord.

Saul is warned that his mission will bring him much suffering, and his trials begin as the synagogue officials of Damascus plot to put him to death (v. 23). Though he is hunted in the city and prevented from exiting the city through its gates, the disciples come to his rescue. In a memorable rescue later mentioned in one of Paul's letters, he is lowered in a basket at night from an opening in the city wall, and he makes his escape (v. 25; 2 Cor. 11:33).

When Saul arrives in Jerusalem, Barnabas acts as his mediator with the leaders of the church. He brings Saul to the apostles and describes how he experienced the risen Jesus and preached his name boldly in Damascus (v. 27). Saul has returned to Jerusalem, beseeching the community he had tried to obliterate for protection. It is critical that the new mission of Saul be rooted in the group of apostles who were with Jesus during his earthly ministry. They represent the tradition that began in Jesus, the Jerusalem community from which the worldwide church would extend.

Both the intensely personal encounter with Jesus that Saul experienced on the road and the apostolic tradition to which he was linked in Jerusalem were necessary for his authentic witness to Jesus. Saul's unique call from Christ and the call of the church were two sides of the same vocation as evangelizer of the nations. Both enthusiasm for the mission and fidelity to the call would continue to impel Saul from Jerusalem to the ends of the earth.

Answer these questions drawn from your reading of the Scripture and the commentary:

‡ Why was it important that Saul begin his proclamation of Jesus in the synagogue?

‡ Why was it important that Saul come to Jerusalem to meet the apostles of Jesus toward the beginning of his Christian mission?

Meditatio

Use your imagination and enter these scenes in Damascus and Jerusalem. Envision what you would experience and how you would respond to these encounters.

✝ What were some of the predominant emotions Saul must have experienced in Damascus and Jerusalem? How did Saul seem to deal with his conflicting feelings?

✝ How did Saul experience forgiveness both from God and from the community he sought to destroy? How did receiving forgiveness empower him to minister both boldly and humbly?

✝ How have I experienced forgiveness for my past mistakes and harmful desires? For what do I need to receive forgiveness in order to serve God with more courage and freedom?

Oratio

Using the images and feelings generated by these Scriptures, spend some time praying to God in words that flow from your heart.

> Saving Lord, I want to serve you and share the Good News of your love with others. Yet, I know that my past mistakes and unhealed wounds prevent me from being a wholehearted disciple. I pray for your merciful forgiveness, and I ask you to help me experience your healing grace.

Continue to pray in whatever words arise from within . . .

Contemplatio

Rest in the embrace of Christ and let yourself feel his complete forgiveness and inner healing. Don't speak or do anything; simply trust.

After a period of wordless contemplation, write a few words about your experience.

Operatio

Saul's personal experience was put into the service of the community. What is God urging me to do for others as a result of my individual encounter with the Bible, the book of the church?

3

Paul Preaches in the
Synagogue on the Sabbath

Lectio

Read the words of Paul's sermon aloud. Listen carefully as if you were hearing the message of Paul proclaimed to his fellow Jews in the synagogue.

ACTS 13:13–31

[13]Then Paul and his companions set sail from Paphos and came to Perga in Pamphylia. John, however, left them and returned to Jerusalem; [14]but they went on from Perga and came to Antioch in Pisidia. And on the sabbath day they went into the synagogue and sat down. [15]After the reading of the law and the prophets, the officials of the synagogue sent them a message, saying, "Brothers, if you have any word of exhortation for the people, give it." [16]So Paul stood up and with a gesture began to speak:

"You Israelites, and others who fear God, listen. [17]The God of this people Israel chose our ancestors and made the people great during their stay in the land of Egypt, and with uplifted arm he led them out of it. [18]For about forty years he put up with them in the wilderness. [19]After he had destroyed seven nations in the land of Canaan, he gave them their land as an inheritance [20]for about four hundred fifty years.

After that he gave them judges until the time of the prophet Samuel. [21]Then they asked for a king; and God gave them Saul son of Kish, a man of the tribe of Benjamin, who reigned for forty years. [22]When he had removed him, he made David their king. In his testimony about him he said, 'I have found David, son of Jesse, to be a man after my heart, who will carry out all my wishes.' [23]Of this man's posterity God has brought to Israel a Savior, Jesus, as he promised; [24]before his coming John had already proclaimed a baptism of repentance to all the people of Israel. [25]And as John was finishing his work, he said, 'What do you suppose that I am? I am not he. No, but one is coming after me; I am not worthy to untie the thong of the sandals on his feet.'

[26]"My brothers, you descendants of Abraham's family, and others who fear God, to us the message of this salvation has been sent. [27]Because the residents of Jerusalem and their leaders did not recognize him or understand the words of the prophets that are read every sabbath, they fulfilled those words by condemning him. [28]Even though they found no cause for a sentence of death, they asked Pilate to have him killed. [29]When they had carried out everything that was written about him, they took him down from the tree and laid him in a tomb. [30]But God raised him from the dead; [31]and for many days he appeared to those who came up with him from Galilee to Jerusalem, and they are now his witnesses to the people."

After hearing Paul's speech with the ear of your heart, continue searching for the significance of his words in the synagogue.

The travel narratives give us a taste of the grueling itinerary of Paul and his companions. Paul journeys on a ship from Paphos on the coast of Cypress to Perga in southern Asia Minor. He then travels northward through the mountainous region to Antioch of Pisidia (vv. 13–14). Luke's narrative makes clear that these unrelenting journeys are impelled by the Holy Spirit and supported by the prayers of the Christian community. In this new stage in the mission, the spread of the gospel picks up speed, as it is destined for the whole world.

As was his practice in every town on his journeys, Paul attends the synagogue service on the Sabbath. Following the readings from the Torah and the prophets, the synagogue officials invite the traveler to speak to the people, and Paul rises to accept the invitation (v. 15). His audience is a mixed group of Jews and "others who fear God," that is, Gentiles who are interested in Judaism.

This first recorded sermon of Paul in Acts is typical of his rabbinical style, interpreting recent events in light of Israel's ancient texts. Paul offers a broad sweep of Israel's grand narrative in order to show how God has acted again to liberate Israel through Jesus the Savior. He recounts the most familiar features of God's unique relationship with Israel: the exodus from Egypt (v. 17), the testing in the wilderness (v. 18), the conquest of the land (v. 19), the period of the judges (v. 20), and the monarchy under Saul and David (vv. 21–22).

Paul's many references to Israel's history come to a climax as he affirms that God's promises to David were answered in the coming of Jesus (v. 23). David was a prefiguring of the Messiah, who was born of David's descendants. Jesus, the new king of God's people, is the promised "Savior" of Israel. Like the prophets of old, John the Baptist was his herald, calling all the people to repentance (vv. 24–25). And now, Paul proclaims, "to us the message of this salvation has been sent" (v. 26).

Paul warns the people that in the days of Jesus the people of Jerusalem did not recognize their Savior, and they failed to understand that the words of the prophets pointed to their Messiah. Instead they condemned him and handed him over to Pilate to be killed, fulfilling the words of the prophets themselves (vv. 27–29). Yet, God raised Jesus from the tomb of death, and he appeared to his disciples, who are now his witnesses.

Paul never separates himself from his own people, the Jews. He places himself among Israel's ancestors, rejoicing in their divine election and promises and grieving at their unfaithfulness to God. Now, the message of salvation has been sent through Paul to the Israelites scattered to all the nations. Paul proclaims the gospel as the fulfillment of the Torah and the prophets, and the response of his audience will determine its destination.

After listening to Paul's inspired sermon, consider this question:

✝ Why is it so necessary to know the Old Testament in order to understand the significance of Jesus?

Meditatio

After considering how Paul's speech was understood by its first hearers, reflect on its significance in your own life and how you may respond.

‡ What moved Paul to travel such distances and to proclaim the gospel so persistently? What parallels do I see in my own sense of mission?

‡ For a prayerful reflection on God's promises to David, read Psalm 89:20–37. Why is the reign of King David the climax of Paul's summary of Israel's history? What do the words of the psalm help me to realize about God, David, and Israel?

‡ Why does Paul recount highlights from Israel's history in order to prepare his listeners for the gospel of Jesus? How does Paul's speech encourage me to study the Hebrew Scriptures?

Oratio

Pray to God in response to the message you have heard in God's Word. You may choose to begin with these or similar words.

God of Abraham, Moses, and David, you have chosen your people and guided them in your way throughout Israel's history. Give me inspiration and courage through the stories of my ancestors in faith, and prepare me to welcome your Son Jesus, our Savior.

Continue to pray as your heart directs . . .

Contemplatio

God has been loving and trustworthy throughout the ages. Trust that God, who is always faithful, will continue to fulfill his promises to you.

After a period of wordless contemplation, write a few words about your experience.

Operatio

What new insight has Paul's speech offered you today? Take that insight with you through the day and apply it to the challenges that face you.

4

God's Universal Mission
to All Nations

Continue speaking the words of Paul aloud and listen carefully for the words addressed to you. Read slowly and mark any words or phrases that strike you personally.

ACTS 13:32–52

[32]"And we bring you the good news that what God promised to our ancestors [33]he has fulfilled for us, their children, by raising Jesus; as also it is written in the second psalm,

'You are my Son;

today I have begotten you.'

[34]As to his raising him from the dead, no more to return to corruption, he has spoken in this way,

'I will give you the holy promises made to David.'

[35]Therefore he has also said in another psalm,

'You will not let your Holy One experience corruption.'

[36]For David, after he had served the purpose of God in his own generation, died, was laid beside his ancestors, and experienced corruption; [37]but he whom God raised up experienced no corruption. [38]Let it be known to you therefore, my brothers, that through this man

forgiveness of sins is proclaimed to you; [39]by this Jesus everyone who believes is set free from all those sins from which you could not be freed by the law of Moses. [40]Beware, therefore, that what the prophets said does not happen to you:

[41]'Look, you scoffers!
Be amazed and perish,
for in your days I am doing a work,
a work that you will never believe, even if someone tells you.' "

[42]As Paul and Barnabas were going out, the people urged them to speak about these things again the next sabbath. [43]When the meeting of the synagogue broke up, many Jews and devout converts to Judaism followed Paul and Barnabas, who spoke to them and urged them to continue in the grace of God.

[44]The next sabbath almost the whole city gathered to hear the word of the Lord. [45]But when the Jews saw the crowds, they were filled with jealousy; and blaspheming, they contradicted what was spoken by Paul. [46]Then both Paul and Barnabas spoke out boldly, saying, "It was necessary that the word of God should be spoken first to you. Since you reject it and judge yourselves to be unworthy of eternal life, we are now turning to the Gentiles. [47]For so the Lord has commanded us, saying,

'I have set you to be a light for the Gentiles,
so that you may bring salvation to the ends of the earth.' "

[48]When the Gentiles heard this, they were glad and praised the word of the Lord; and as many as had been destined for eternal life became believers. [49]Thus the word of the Lord spread throughout the region. [50]But the Jews incited the devout women of high standing and the leading men of the city, and stirred up persecution against Paul and Barnabas, and drove them out of their region. [51]So they shook the dust off their feet in protest against them, and went to Iconium. [52]And the disciples were filled with joy and with the Holy Spirit.

After allowing Paul's sermon to penetrate your mind and heart, continue searching for the significance of these ancient words of Scripture.

Two elements form the foundation of Paul's preaching: first, the tradition of what Jesus said and did, as handed down through the church by the apostles, and second, the ancient Scriptures of Israel that were fulfilled through the coming of Jesus. "What God promised" is expressed through those Scriptures, and what God "has fulfilled" is expressed through the life, death, and resurrection of Jesus (vv. 32–33). Through citing ancient texts referring originally to David, Paul shows his audience that what God promised David is now given to the present generation in Jesus.

Paul pulls together quotations from the Psalms as a demonstration that the resurrection of Jesus is the complete fulfillment of God's promise to raise up an eternal heir to the throne of David. Paul then contrasts what is possible "by the law of Moses" and what can be achieved through Jesus. Through him God has offered forgiveness and freedom from sin to everyone who believes (vv. 38–39). Finally, Paul ends his sermon with a warning to his hearers by quoting from the prophet Habakkuk (vv. 40–41). In the days of the prophet, the people failed to recognize what was happening as the work of God. Paul tells his audience in the synagogue that they must not scoff at the gospel message they are hearing but must respond with faith in Christ.

Paul's speech receives a positive response, and the people urge him to return the next Sabbath. Many Jews follow Paul, and he urges them to "continue in the grace of God" (vv. 42–43). On the next Sabbath, huge crowds gather to listen, stirring many of the Jewish leaders to jealousy because the Gentiles are now beginning to share the faith of Israel (vv. 44–45). They contradict Paul, reject his inclusive message, and begin to stir up a persecution.

In response, Paul speaks out boldly, demonstrating how his mission from the Lord is a response to the words of Isaiah: "I have set you to be a light for the Gentiles, so that you may bring salvation to the ends of the earth" (v. 47; see Isa. 49:6). Though it was to be the role of Israel to tell the people of the world about God's salvation, many of them are rejecting that role because of their ingrained animosity toward the Gentiles.

From this point on, Paul turns increasingly to the Gentiles, though he never turns his back on the people of Israel. In nearly every city of his travels, he goes first to the Jews, and when turned away by one synagogue, he goes to another. He knows that the covenant benefits were promised first to his own people, and he never ceases to identify himself with them. Yet, he is also the apostle to the Gentiles, called to bring the message of salvation to all the nations of the earth.

Meditatio

‡ What does Paul say is the primary effect of Christ's resurrection for his listeners (vv. 38–39)? What does this mean to me?

‡ What are some of the emotional responses created by Paul's sermon among the various groups in the city? Why does Paul's message produce such a variety of responses?

‡ Paul's quotation of Isaiah 49:6 in verse 47 is a programmatic verse for the remainder of Acts. How does this describe the mission of the church today? How do I fit into that mission?

Oratio

Speak to God in response to your lectio and meditatio.

> Saving Lord, you have raised up Jesus your Son as the answer to your covenant promises to Israel. He is the light for all the nations so that salvation will come to all peoples. Help me to listen carefully to your Word so that I may be a bearer of your gospel in the world.

Continue to pray, using whatever words and phrases of the text most touched your heart . . .

Contemplatio

Know that God wants you to share in all the blessings of the covenant. Ask for the gift of faith; trust that God will enfold you with his grace.

After a period of trusting silence, write a few words about your experience.

Operatio

In what way is God calling me to be a light to the nations today? In what way can I bring light to a person or situation in need of God's joy and grace?

5

Good News
of the Living God

Engage your senses as you read the text. Imagine the sights, colors, sounds, smells, and textures of the scene. Use the sensory descriptions to ground you in the drama of the scene.

ACTS 14:8–18

[8]In Lystra there was a man sitting who could not use his feet and had never walked, for he had been crippled from birth. [9]He listened to Paul as he was speaking. And Paul, looking at him intently and seeing that he had faith to be healed, [10]said in a loud voice, "Stand upright on your feet." And the man sprang up and began to walk. [11]When the crowds saw what Paul had done, they shouted in the Lycaonian language, "The gods have come down to us in human form!" [12]Barnabas they called Zeus, and Paul they called Hermes, because he was the chief speaker. [13]The priest of Zeus, whose temple was just outside the city, brought oxen and garlands to the gates; he and the crowds wanted to offer sacrifice. [14]When the apostles Barnabas and Paul heard of it, they tore their clothes and rushed out into the crowd, shouting, [15]"Friends, why are you doing this? We are mortals

just like you, and we bring you good news, that you should turn from these worthless things to the living God, who made the heaven and the earth and the sea and all that is in them. [16]In past generations he allowed all the nations to follow their own ways; [17]yet he has not left himself without a witness in doing good—giving you rains from heaven and fruitful seasons, and filling you with food and your hearts with joy." [18]Even with these words, they scarcely restrained the crowds from offering sacrifice to them.

Feel the impact of the Scripture upon you and then continue your listening through the reflection of the church.

Paul's mission to evangelize the Gentiles becomes more explicit in the dramatic events at Lystra. This town seems to have no synagogue and is the site for Paul's first encounter with a purely Gentile audience. Because his audience is not Jewish, Paul's missionary method is significantly different. He speaks in the forum, which is the marketplace and site for public concourse. Here Paul addresses the crowds, and the lame beggar listens to him (v. 9).

Paul's healing of the lame man resembles Peter's healing of the lame man in Jerusalem (Acts 3:1–16), continuing the frequent parallels between the work of Peter and Paul. Their healings continue the tradition of Jesus, who healed a lame man as a sign of his saving power (Luke 5:17–26). But Luke includes this healing account of Paul in order to express an even deeper meaning. The man's helplessness and inability to move on his own signify the human condition in need of salvation. After speaking, Paul understands that the man has "faith to be healed." The lame man perceives the power of God in Paul's words and opens himself to God's transforming authority. Weak and unable to do anything in his own power, the man expresses the trusting conviction of faith and experiences God's saving strength.

The crowds witness Paul's command to "stand upright," and their response to the healing is overwhelmingly positive (vv. 10–11). Thinking that Barnabas is Zeus, the principal god of the Greeks, and Paul is Hermes, the messenger god who governs speech, the people express their gratitude for the saving message of Paul through their own pagan practices. The priest of the town brings oxen and garlands to perform a grand sacrifice for these gods in human form (v. 13). When the news reaches Paul and Barnabas about what the people are doing, they tear their clothes as an expression of their distress and rush into the crowd to protest their action.

The brief summary of Paul's address to the people continues to demonstrate his approach to evangelizing Gentiles (vv. 15–17). Rather than beginning with the Hebrew Scriptures as he had in the synagogues, Paul begins with philosophy and natural theology. Instead of showing that Jesus is the Messiah of Israel as he had with the Jews, he begins with the existence of the one God who is the principal cause of all things, which is the heart of Jewish monotheism. This "living God" is the one who creates and sustains all things in existence. The activity of God in nature, making the crops fruitful and bringing joy to human hearts, is a "witness" to God's goodness. Paul explains that in the past God allowed all people to follow their own gods and beliefs. Now, however, is the time to offer the Good News of the living God to all the nations.

Answer these questions based on your reading of the text and commentary:

✝ What are some of the differences between Paul's approach to the Jews and his approach to the Gentiles?

✝ What deeper meaning does Luke desire to express in the healing of the lame man?

Meditatio

Think about the deeper implications of this Scripture passage on your understanding and living the faith.

‡ Why do Paul and Barnabas object so strongly to the actions of the townspeople of Lystra? Why is it important to attribute power to its divine source rather than its human instruments?

‡ Why is faith so critically important for the healing of the lame man? How does this narrative help me reflect on my condition before God?

‡ How does Paul demonstrate the existence of the "living God" to the pagan believers? What does Paul add to his argument in Romans 1:20?

Oratio

Offer praise to God for the wondrous ways he is revealed to you as the Creator and Sustainer of the world.

Merciful God, you are the cause of all things, and you lovingly sustain all things in existence with your power. Help me to look in wonder at your creation and gladden my heart with the knowledge of your providence. May I always continue to give you praise.

Continue this prayer by naming the reasons for your praise and thanks . . .

Contemplatio

Take some time to look in all directions at the world around you. Spend some silent time in gratitude for God's creative love.

After a period of grateful quiet, write a few words about your experience.

Operatio

How is God offering me healing today? Is my faith ready to accept what God wants to do in my life? How can I prepare for God's saving action within me?

6

The Church in Jerusalem
Welcomes the Gentiles

Lectio

Kiss the sacred text of Scripture as a sign of honor to God's Word within it.
Ask the Holy Spirit to guide your listening and understanding.

ACTS 15:1–6, 12–21

¹Then certain individuals came down from Judea and were teaching the brothers, "Unless you are circumcised according to the custom of Moses, you cannot be saved." ²And after Paul and Barnabas had no small dissension and debate with them, Paul and Barnabas and some of the others were appointed to go up to Jerusalem to discuss this question with the apostles and the elders. ³So they were sent on their way by the church, and as they passed through both Phoenicia and Samaria, they reported the conversion of the Gentiles, and brought great joy to all the believers. ⁴When they came to Jerusalem, they were welcomed by the church and the apostles and the elders, and they reported all that God had done with them. ⁵But some believers who belonged to the sect of the Pharisees stood up and said, "It is necessary for them to be circumcised and ordered to keep the law of Moses."

⁶The apostles and the elders met together to consider this matter.

¹²The whole assembly kept silence, and listened to Barnabas and Paul as they told of all the signs and wonders that God had done through them among the Gentiles. ¹³After they finished speaking, James replied, "My brothers, listen to me. ¹⁴Simeon has related how God first looked favorably on the Gentiles, to take from among them a people for his name. ¹⁵This agrees with the words of the prophets, as it is written,

¹⁶'After this I will return,
and I will rebuild the dwelling of David, which has fallen;
from its ruins I will rebuild it,
and I will set it up,
¹⁷so that all other peoples may seek the Lord—
even all the Gentiles over whom my name has been called.
Thus says the Lord, who has been making these things ¹⁸known from long ago.'

¹⁹Therefore I have reached the decision that we should not trouble those Gentiles who are turning to God, ²⁰but we should write to them to abstain only from things polluted by idols and from fornication and from whatever has been strangled and from blood. ²¹For in every city, for generations past, Moses has had those who proclaim him, for he has been read aloud every sabbath in the synagogues."

After listening to the words of the church as recorded in Scripture, listen also to the words of the church's interpretation through teaching and scholarship.

For the earliest disciples of Jesus, following the law of Moses was not an issue. As faithful Jews, Jesus and his disciples lived the precepts of the Torah in obedience to God's ancient covenant with Israel. The church's first major crisis came as non-Jews began to respond to the gospel and believe in Jesus as Savior. It seemed natural to some Jewish Christians that receiving the sign of circumcision, following dietary instructions, and observing other precepts of the law would be required for anyone to come into the community of God's people. If the Gentiles were to participate in the blessings of the covenant, surely they must be faithful to the Torah of Israel.

Some of the Jewish Christians, especially the converts from the party of the Pharisees, sought to enforce their belief throughout the church: "Unless you are circumcised according to the custom of Moses, you cannot be saved" (v. 1). Paul and Barnabas, in contrast, had seen what God was doing among the Gentiles and were convinced that Gentiles should not be required to become Jews in order to become Christians. The crisis became so urgent that Paul and Barnabas were commissioned to travel to Jerusalem to discuss the issue with the apostles and elders (v. 2).

At this Jerusalem council there was much discussion among the leaders of the church over these questions. Finally, in a remarkable display of unity, James defended the position expressed by Paul and Peter, that God was truly at work in the mission to the Gentiles and that God was making of them "a people for his name" (v. 14). He appealed to Scripture to demonstrate how the law and the prophets are fulfilled as the covenant promises are extended to all people. He quoted the prophet Amos to demonstrate that the restored kingdom of Israel would include people of all nations, "so that all other peoples may seek the Lord—even all the Gentiles" (v. 17).

The final decree of the Jerusalem council asked only four things of the Gentiles: that they should abstain from things polluted by idols, from sexual immorality, from eating strangled animals, and from the blood of any creature (v. 20). These are taken from part of the Torah's holiness code (Lev. 17–18). These minimal requirements had always bound not only the Israelites but also the foreigners who chose to live among them. James insisted on these stipulations so that the Jewish and Gentile Christians could share table fellowship and live in harmony with one another. These prohibitions would remind the new Gentile believers that they were being welcomed into a church that was rooted in Israel and founded on the Torah (v. 21).

Synthesize your listening by responding to this question:

‡ What factors led the church leaders to their decision?

Meditatio

After trying to understand the church in its formative stages, think about the implications of this passage for the church today and for your own discipleship.

‡ What can we learn from the apostolic council in Jerusalem about how the church is called to teach the faith today? What lessons can be learned from these apostles?

‡ Dissension and debate seem to be a legitimate and necessary element in the early Christian community. How can disagreement and dispute be important elements in personal and communal discernment?

‡ What can I learn from these apostles of the early church about problem solving and decision making? What principles could I apply in my own life?

Oratio

We can be confident that God cares about every aspect of our lives and listens to our prayer.

God of the covenant, you began your church on the foundation of the apostles and their witness to Jesus. We are privileged to share in the tradition we received from them and to continue to build the church today. May we continue to seek the truth in love.

Continue to pray from your heart . . .

Contemplatio

After words are no longer necessary or helpful, just relax in the presence of God.

After a period of contemplative silence, write a few words about your experience.

Operatio

How effective am I as a witness to my faith? What can I do to invite and welcome new members into the family of Christ?

7

Paul Proclaims the God of
All in Athens

Lectio

*Vocalize the words of this text so that you not only read them with your eyes
but also hear them with your ears. Listen carefully to these inspired words.*

ACTS 17:16–31

[16]While Paul was waiting for them in Athens, he was deeply distressed to see that the city was full of idols. [17]So he argued in the synagogue with the Jews and the devout persons, and also in the marketplace every day with those who happened to be there. [18]Also some Epicurean and Stoic philosophers debated with him. Some said, "What does this babbler want to say?" Others said, "He seems to be a proclaimer of foreign divinities." (This was because he was telling the good news about Jesus and the resurrection.) [19]So they took him and brought him to the Areopagus and asked him, "May we know what this new teaching is that you are presenting? [20]It sounds rather strange to us, so we would like to know what it means." [21]Now all the Athenians and the foreigners living there would spend their time in nothing but telling or hearing something new.

[22]Then Paul stood in front of the Areopagus and said, "Athenians, I see how extremely religious you are in every way. [23]For as I went

41

through the city and looked carefully at the objects of your worship, I found among them an altar with the inscription, 'To an unknown god.' What therefore you worship as unknown, this I proclaim to you. [24]The God who made the world and everything in it, he who is Lord of heaven and earth, does not live in shrines made by human hands, [25]nor is he served by human hands, as though he needed anything, since he himself gives to all mortals life and breath and all things. [26]From one ancestor he made all nations to inhabit the whole earth, and he allotted the times of their existence and the boundaries of the places where they would live, [27]so that they would search for God and perhaps grope for him and find him—though indeed he is not far from each one of us. [28]For 'In him we live and move and have our being'; as even some of your own poets have said,

'For we too are his offspring.'

[29]Since we are God's offspring, we ought not to think that the deity is like gold, or silver, or stone, an image formed by the art and imagination of mortals. [30]While God has overlooked the times of human ignorance, now he commands all people everywhere to repent, [31]because he has fixed a day on which he will have the world judged in righteousness by a man whom he has appointed, and of this he has given assurance to all by raising him from the dead."

Let the speech of Paul penetrate your mind and heart, and then continue to explore the meaning of this scene through this commentary.

Though the most glorious days of Athens have passed, the city is filled with fine examples of art and architecture, and it is still considered the intellectual capital of the Greco-Roman world. Athens is a cosmopolitan city, and Paul would have encountered quite a diversity of people, from the Jews who met in the synagogue to the great variety of peoples from many nations whom he encountered in the marketplace (v. 17).

As Paul walks through the Acropolis, the agora, and the many streets of Athens, he sees the representations of various gods in the temples, in the niches of buildings, and on street corners. As a monotheistic Jew, Paul sees these not as objects of art but as idolatry, and he is deeply distressed by them. As Paul contends with audiences both in the synagogue and in the marketplace, his message is misunderstood. They accuse him of being a "babbler," literally one who picks up bits of news as a bird pecks at seeds, and "a proclaimer of foreign divinities," perhaps because he spoke of Jesus and resurrection (v. 18), which sounded to his hearers like a pair of new gods (in Greek, *Iesous* and *Anastasis*).

Finally, Paul is brought to the Areopagus, the most venerable institution in Athens, legendary for hearing matters of legal, political, and religious significance. The philosophers and people of Athens ask Paul to explain his new teaching, and Paul fashions his response in a well-constructed piece of classical rhetoric. He interprets the many temples and statues of the city as a genuine search for the divine and an expression of the human impulse to worship (vv. 22–23). His notice of an altar "To an unknown god" (v. 23) becomes his springboard for proclaiming "the God who made the world and everything in it, he who is Lord of heaven and earth" (v. 24).

In this scene, Luke offers us a model of how Jerusalem can speak to Athens, how divine revelation contained in the Scriptures can dialogue with the human reason of philosophy and natural theology. Paul uses Greek writers as legitimate conversation partners in approaching the truth of the gospel. However, speculative thinking can move people only to the borders of faith in the gospel. The God of all people, about whom Paul has been speaking, is also the living and personal God revealed in the Scriptures of Israel. Before this God all people must repent and come to believe. Paul concludes his speech by asserting that the resurrection of Jesus from the dead is humanity's assurance that this God is indeed Lord of heaven and earth.

After listening to Paul, consider how the Athenians might have heard what Paul was saying.

‡ Which words of Paul might have had the most positive impact on his audience in Athens?

Meditatio

Think about Paul's work among the people of Athens in terms of your own search for God and the meaning of life.

✝ What are some of the positive signs Paul saw in Athens? In what ways do these express the searching and longing of people today?

✝ What truths about God did the Greek philosophers and poets express? What words of the Athenian thinkers help me as I seek to understand the existence of God?

✝ How can Paul's work in Athens be an example or model of Christian dialogue with other religions and the secular world today?

Oratio

Speak to God in response to the words, ideas, and images contained in your reading of this scene from Acts.

God of the entire world, you have instilled in all people a natural hunger and longing for you. Help me to recognize that my own heart is searching, and show me ways to seek out the lost and the restless hearts of others.

Continue to pray to God in your own words . . .

Contemplatio

Realize that God is "not far from each of us." Relax in the God in whom "we live and move and have our being."

After a period of quiet contemplation, write a few words about your experience.

Operatio

What are some effective ways I can evangelize without sounding preachy? What one person could I bring closer to God today through their own natural longing and curiosity?

8

Paul Sparks a Riot in Ephesus

Lectio

Read the passage carefully, pausing to imagine the scene. Think about the sights and sounds as well as the emotions of the characters and the confusion of the uprising.

ACTS 19:23–39

²³About that time no little disturbance broke out concerning the Way. ²⁴A man named Demetrius, a silversmith who made silver shrines of Artemis, brought no little business to the artisans. ²⁵These he gathered together, with the workers of the same trade, and said, "Men, you know that we get our wealth from this business. ²⁶You also see and hear that not only in Ephesus but in almost the whole of Asia this Paul has persuaded and drawn away a considerable number of people by saying that gods made with hands are not gods. ²⁷And there is danger not only that this trade of ours may come into disrepute but also that the temple of the great goddess Artemis will be scorned, and she will be deprived of her majesty that brought all Asia and the world to worship her."

²⁸When they heard this, they were enraged and shouted, "Great is Artemis of the Ephesians!" ²⁹The city was filled with the confusion; and people rushed together to the theater, dragging with them Gaius and Aristarchus, Macedonians who were Paul's travel companions. ³⁰Paul wished to go into the crowd, but the disciples would not let him; ³¹even some officials of the province of Asia, who were friendly to him, sent him a message urging him not to venture into the theater. ³²Meanwhile, some were shouting one thing, some another; for the assembly was in confusion, and most of them did not know why they had come together. ³³Some of the crowd gave instructions to Alexander, whom the Jews had pushed forward. And Alexander motioned for silence and tried to make a defense before the people. ³⁴But when they recognized that he was a Jew, for about two hours all of them shouted in unison, "Great is Artemis of the Ephesians!" ³⁵But when the town clerk had quieted the crowd, he said, "Citizens of Ephesus, who is there that does not know that the city of the Ephesians is the temple keeper of the great Artemis and of the statue that fell from heaven? ³⁶Since these things cannot be denied, you ought to be quiet and do nothing rash. ³⁷You have brought these men here who are neither temple robbers nor blasphemers of our goddess. ³⁸If therefore Demetrius and the artisans with him have a complaint against anyone, the courts are open, and there are proconsuls; let them bring charges there against one another. ³⁹If there is anything further you want to know, it must be settled in the regular assembly."

After imagining this scene through the words of the text, continue to search for the full meaning of this passage.

The riot in Ephesus depicts what happens when the gospel of Jesus dares to disturb the real-world financial and political concerns of a city. In one of the liveliest scenes of Acts, Luke demonstrates how the greed, acquisitiveness, and self-protection of the city's inhabitants combine to produce violent emotions, noise and confusion, throngs in the streets, and mob justice.

Artemis, the multi-breasted, fertile mother goddess, was the principal deity worshipped at Ephesus. Her temple was four times the size of the Parthenon at Athens and designated as one of the seven wonders of the ancient world. The description in Acts suggests a widespread belief that her image "fell from heaven" (v. 35). Archaeologists have uncovered silver statues of the goddess, coins with representations of her temple, and terra-cotta reproductions of the temple. Her festivals in Ephesus attracted thousands of visitors and were the city's primary economic industry.

A silversmith named Demetrius, who crafted silver shrines to Artemis, called together the artisans of the city who made their living from crafts related to the cult of Artemis. He knew that Paul's message was a threat to their livelihood (vv. 24–25). If Paul persuaded people throughout the region that "gods made with hands are not gods" (v. 26), then not only was their trade at risk but the temple of Artemis could also be scorned.

Demetrius knew how to stir up a crowd and appealed to the religious devotion of the Ephesians: the great goddess "will be deprived of her majesty that brought all Asia and the world to worship her" (v. 27). The message of the gospel for all nations seemed to be in direct conflict with the religion, culture, and economy of Ephesus. The crowd was furious and chanted, "Great is Artemis of the Ephesians!" (v. 28). They spilled into the streets, shouting and gathering more people as they went, converging in the huge and acoustically perfect amphitheater of Ephesus. Paul was urged not to go to the theater, and he seems to have escaped from the mob.

In describing this scene, Luke wished to contrast the chaos created by the followers of the pagan gods with the peaceful order produced by Paul and the Christian disciples. The assembly in the theater is characterized by idolatry, anxiety, greed, and concern for profit, whereas the Christian assembly throughout Acts is depicted as united in mind and heart, witnessing their faith, joined at table, and sharing possessions.

After reading the text of the riot in Ephesus, consider this question:

‡ Why was the gospel that Paul preached so threatening to the silversmiths and other artisans of Ephesus?

Meditatio

Imagine how you would respond to the encounter in Ephesus and consider its implications for Christian life today.

‡ In Ephesus the worship of Artemis became the source of the city's economic gain. What are some of the positive and negative implications of this tendency in religion? Does Christianity do the same?

‡ What are some examples in which the gospel of Jesus challenges the financial and political concerns of our society today?

‡ Some of today's cultural idols are money, success, power, and possessions. How does my Christian faith affect my relationship with these idols?

Oratio

Express the thoughts and feelings that arise within you after reading this Scripture passage and address them to God.

Lord Jesus, you have come into our world and have shown us how to exist in the midst of the idols that surround us. Teach us how to honor the invisible God of all creation and to seek first the kingdom of God.

Continue to pray to God from your heart in whatever words you wish . . .

Contemplatio

In contrast to the noisy confusion of the scene in Ephesus, spend some quiet moments resting in the peace that only God can bring to you.

After a period of quiet contemplation, write a few words about your experience.

Operatio

What is one way I can transfer my loyalty today from a cultural idol to the Lord of my life? What kind of support do I need to turn away from idols?

9

Paul Bids Farewell
to the Churches

Lectio

Close off the distractions around you and enter a moment of stillness.
Breathe in, being filled with the presence of God's Spirit. Breathe out, letting
go of all that could distract you from this sacred time.

ACTS 20:7–24

[7]On the first day of the week, when we met to break bread, Paul was holding a discussion with them; since he intended to leave the next day, he continued speaking until midnight. [8]There were many lamps in the room upstairs where we were meeting. [9]A young man named Eutychus, who was sitting in the window, began to sink off into a deep sleep while Paul talked still longer. Overcome by sleep, he fell to the ground three floors below and was picked up dead. [10]But Paul went down, and bending over him took him in his arms, and said, "Do not be alarmed, for his life is in him." [11]Then Paul went upstairs, and after he had broken bread and eaten, he continued to converse with them until dawn; then he left. [12]Meanwhile they had taken the boy away alive and were not a little comforted.

¹³We went ahead to the ship and set sail for Assos, intending to take Paul on board there; for he had made this arrangement, intending to go by land himself. ¹⁴When he met us in Assos, we took him on board and went to Mitylene. ¹⁵We sailed from there, and on the following day we arrived opposite Chios. The next day we touched at Samos, and the day after that we came to Miletus. ¹⁶For Paul had decided to sail past Ephesus, so that he might not have to spend time in Asia; he was eager to be in Jerusalem, if possible, on the day of Pentecost.

¹⁷From Miletus he sent a message to Ephesus, asking the elders of the church to meet him. ¹⁸When they came to him, he said to them:

"You yourselves know how I lived among you the entire time from the first day that I set foot in Asia, ¹⁹serving the Lord with all humility and with tears, enduring the trials that came to me through the plots of the Jews. ²⁰I did not shrink from doing anything helpful, proclaiming the message to you and teaching you publicly and from house to house, ²¹as I testified to both Jews and Greeks about repentance toward God and faith toward our Lord Jesus. ²²And now, as a captive to the Spirit, I am on my way to Jerusalem, not knowing what will happen to me there, ²³except that the Holy Spirit testifies to me in every city that imprisonment and persecutions are waiting for me. ²⁴But I do not count my life of any value to myself, if only I may finish my course and the ministry that I received from the Lord Jesus, to testify to the good news of God's grace."

After reading Paul's affectionate and determined words with the ear of your heart, listen for further understanding as you read the commentary.

Unlike previous scenes that depicted Paul moving outward, preaching to Jews and Gentiles, and making disciples, these scenes show Paul with communities of Christians he has grown to love. Paul continued to gather in synagogues on the Sabbath, but here is clear evidence that Sunday has become the Christian day of worship. "The first day of the week" (v. 7) was the day of the Lord's resurrection, when the community would assemble to celebrate Eucharist.

At this particular service, Paul's preaching and teaching went long into the night because he was leaving them the next morning. A youth named Eutychus, whose name means "good fortune" or "lucky," was sitting in the window of the third floor room in which the church was meeting. Because of the late hour, the many oil lamps that depleted the room's oxygen, and Paul's incessant sermon, Eutychus went to sleep and fell to the ground (v. 9). Paul then descended to the boy, embraced him, and pronounced him alive (v. 10). This miracle account of the boy's resuscitation is rightly set in the context of Sunday worship, when the community remembers the dying and rising of Jesus and his invitation to new life.

As Paul continues his long and final journey to Jerusalem, he desires to meet with the leaders of the church in Ephesus before he leaves them (v. 17). Summoning them to Miletus near the coast, he offers them a heartfelt final address. The parallels between Paul's address and the farewell discourse of Jesus with his disciples are numerous (Luke 22:14–38). Like Jesus, the "one who serves," Paul presents the pattern of his own life as a model for their imitation. He warns them about the difficulties that lie ahead and prepares them for the suffering to come.

Like Jesus, Paul predicts his own passion while on his way to Jerusalem. He walks the path to suffering "a captive to the Spirit" (v. 22). The former persecutor who wanted to bring bound captives to Jerusalem is now a captive of God's Spirit, divinely compelled to move toward that city. There imprisonment and persecution await him (v. 23). Just as the dark clouds gathered during the final chapters of Jesus's journey, we know that Paul's life too will come to a somber end with trial and affliction. He knows he has been called to suffer on behalf of the gospel he preaches. Indeed, as Jesus said of him at his conversion, "I myself will show him how much he must suffer for the sake of my name" (9:16).

Paul's only desire is to finish the course, to complete the task given to him by the risen Lord (v. 24). "The good news of God's grace" summarizes Paul's proclamation to the nations. He is willing to forego even life itself for the sake of that saving gospel.

After reading the story of Paul's farewell, consider this question:

✝ What have I learned about Paul's character in these departure narratives?

Meditatio

Think about the words and actions of Paul as he bid farewell to the communities he had grown to love.

‡ What do I most admire and desire to imitate from the life and ministry of Paul?

‡ Reflect on Paul's words concerning the Lord's Supper (1 Cor. 10:16–17; 11:23–26). What does Paul help me to understand about the communal experience of Eucharist?

‡ What do I want to accomplish at any cost? How does my goal compare to the desire of Paul as expressed in verse 24?

Oratio

Express the thoughts and feelings that arise within you after reading this Scripture passage and address them to God.

> Suffering Lord, you called Paul to the ministry of proclaiming your Good News to the world. Give me a taste of his passionate zeal for the gospel and give me the courage to strive toward my life's goal. Make me too "a captive to the Spirit" as I seek to follow your way.

Continue to pray to God from your heart in whatever words you wish . . .

Contemplatio

Spend some quiet moments pondering the love Paul had for his community. Ask God to instill the gift of that love in your life.

After a period of quiet contemplation, write a few words about your experience.

Operatio

Write out a short mission statement stating your life's purpose and goal. What is one way I can consciously live that mission today?

10

Paul Urges the Churches
to Be Ready and Alert

Lectio

Continue reading Paul's farewell address, feeling Paul's zeal and love for his companions in the gospel.

ACTS 20:25–38

[25]"And now I know that none of you, among whom I have gone about proclaiming the kingdom, will ever see my face again. [26]Therefore I declare to you this day that I am not responsible for the blood of any of you, [27]for I did not shrink from declaring to you the whole purpose of God. [28]Keep watch over yourselves and over all the flock, of which the Holy Spirit has made you overseers, to shepherd the church of God that he obtained with the blood of his own Son. [29]I know that after I have gone, savage wolves will come in among you, not sparing the flock. [30]Some even from your own group will come distorting the truth in order to entice the disciples to follow them. [31]Therefore be alert, remembering that for three years I did not cease night or day to warn everyone with tears. [32]And now I commend you to God and to the message of his grace, a message that is able to build you up and to give you the inheritance among all who are sanctified. [33]I coveted

no one's silver or gold or clothing. [34]You know for yourselves that I worked with my own hands to support myself and my companions. [35]In all this I have given you an example that by such work we must support the weak, remembering the words of the Lord Jesus, for he himself said, 'It is more blessed to give than to receive.'"

[36]When he had finished speaking, he knelt down with them all and prayed. [37]There was much weeping among them all; they embraced Paul and kissed him, [38]grieving especially because of what he had said, that they would not see him again. Then they brought him to the ship.

After allowing the words of Paul's farewell to touch your heart, continue to explore the significance of this scene.

The scene of Paul's farewell speech to the Ephesian elders demonstrates greater feeling than any passage in Acts. It offers an intimate portrait of Paul that the frenzied pace of activity and travel has not allowed up to this point. Paul expresses here his deep love for the people of the church in Ephesus and his intense desire that their leaders guard them from harm and guide them in the way of Jesus.

As is typical in the farewell speeches of the Bible, Paul addresses words of counsel to his successors in the church's leadership. He makes clear that ministry in the church is not just a matter of teaching God's truth but of embodying that truth. The exemplary lives of Christ's ministers testify to the genuineness of the gospel. Paul urges the church's leaders to be models to those under their care, and he offers himself as an example for their imitation. The church always needs its saints, models of holy living and dying.

The pastoral care of the Ephesian church is the center of Paul's concern. Presuming that he will not see them again, he states that his conscience is clear if any of them fall away (vv. 25–27). He proclaimed the kingdom and did all he could to teach them "the whole purpose of God" from God's call to Abraham to the formation of "the church of God that he obtained with the blood of his own Son" (v. 28). Paul's pastoral role has now ended, and the Ephesian elders are to carry on as shepherds of the flock.

Paul stresses both the sacredness and the precariousness of the elders' task. They have been given their task as "overseers" of the flock by the Holy Spirit. The pastoral metaphor of shepherds caring for the flock is extended with the image of the "savage wolves." These dangers to the flock come both from outside (v. 29) and from within (v. 30) the church. False teachers and unworthy leaders will seduce the church and draw disciples to themselves rather than to Christ.

Paul connects the example of his own ministry and his exhortation to the elders with the life of Jesus, the ultimate model for imitation. He offers a saying of Jesus not recorded in any of the four Gospels: "It is more blessed to give than to receive" (v. 35). Church leaders have a responsibility to give of themselves and to "support the weak" after the model of Jesus the Shepherd.

This farewell speech foreshadows the end of Paul's missionary activities and hints at his suffering and future martyrdom for Christ. The final leave-taking involves praying, weeping, embracing, kissing, and grieving (vv. 36–38). This emotional scene expresses the deep affection that must bind together every Christian community and the sense of loving responsibility passed from the generation of the apostles to the leaders of the church in every age.

After considering Paul's farewell to the church, respond to these questions about the text:

‡ Which characteristics of Paul's ministry does he offer as an example to the elders of Ephesus?

‡ Describe the way that Paul uses the images of shepherd, flock, and wolves to urge church leaders to "keep watch" (v. 28).

Meditatio

Use your imagination to enter the scene of Paul's emotional departure. Allow this scene to interact with your own care and hope for the church and its future.

‡ Paul urges the Ephesian elders to "keep watch" (v. 28) and "be alert" (v. 31). What does Paul mean by these two imperatives?

‡ What is the role of God, his Son, and the Holy Spirit in the ministry to which the elders are appointed (v. 28)? How does the trinitarian God guide my understanding of discipleship?

‡ Why would the elders have grieved so emotionally at Paul's departure? What would they miss most about Paul?

Oratio

Be aware of the feelings that have arisen within you while imagining this emotional scene and express them in prayer to God.

Good Shepherd, you have called people in every age to guide and keep watch over your church. Help me to follow the example of Paul and his pastoral support for the weak. Give me a passionate desire to give of myself to others and to care for those in need.

Continue to pray to God from your heart in whatever words you wish . . .

Contemplatio

Spend some time slowly repeating the words of Jesus: "It is more blessed to give than to receive." Realize that God is transforming you from the inside out without your awareness.

After a period of quiet contemplation, write a few words about your experience.

Operatio

1 What is one way that God has been molding me through my contemplatio?
2 How can I be aware of that change throughout my day?

11

Paul Welcomed by the Church in Jerusalem

Lectio

Read the passage slowly and carefully. As you read the Scripture and commentary, note any words or phrases that strike you.

ACTS 21:10–14, 17–26

[10]While we were staying [in Caesarea] for several days, a prophet named Agabus came down from Judea. [11]He came to us and took Paul's belt, bound his own feet and hands with it, and said, "Thus says the Holy Spirit, 'This is the way the Jews in Jerusalem will bind the man who owns this belt and will hand him over to the Gentiles.'" [12]When we heard this, we and the people there urged him not to go up to Jerusalem. [13]Then Paul answered, "What are you doing, weeping and breaking my heart? For I am ready not only to be bound but even to die in Jerusalem for the name of the Lord Jesus." [14]Since he would not be persuaded, we remained silent except to say, "The Lord's will be done."

[17]When we arrived in Jerusalem, the brothers welcomed us warmly. [18]The next day Paul went with us to visit James; and all the elders were present. [19]After greeting them, he related one by one the things

that God had done among the Gentiles through his ministry. [20]When they heard it, they praised God. Then they said to him, "You see, brother, how many thousands of believers there are among the Jews, and they are all zealous for the law. [21]They have been told about you that you teach all the Jews living among the Gentiles to forsake Moses, and that you tell them not to circumcise their children or observe the customs. [22]What then is to be done? They will certainly hear that you have come. [23]So do what we tell you. We have four men who are under a vow. [24]Join these men, go through the rite of purification with them, and pay for the shaving of their heads. Thus all will know that there is nothing in what they have been told about you, but that you yourself observe and guard the law. [25]But as for the Gentiles who have become believers, we have sent a letter with our judgment that they should abstain from what has been sacrificed to idols and from blood and from what is strangled and from fornication." [26]Then Paul took the men, and the next day, having purified himself, he entered the temple with them, making public the completion of the days of purification when the sacrifice would be made for each of them.

After carefully reading this text, continue to explore its meaning and message through the following description:

Paul's final journey to Jerusalem parallels that of Jesus. The sense of foreboding is expressed by the prophet Agabus (vv. 10–11). Like the ancient prophets Jeremiah and Ezekiel, Agabus expresses his prophecy through symbolic gestures. He uses Paul's belt to enact the oracle he speaks. The prophecy echoes Jesus's own predictions of his passion in the Gospels: he will be bound and handed over to the Gentiles.

As in the previous farewell speech of Paul, the emotional intensity of the scene is high. Paul has generated love and loyalty among his followers. Despite the weeping and urging of his companions that he not go to Jerusalem, Paul is determined to follow the Lord's will and continue his journey to the holy city (vv. 12–13). Paul's anguish does not deter him from expressing his willingness to suffer and even to die "for the name of the Lord Jesus" (v. 13).

Narrating Paul's arrival in Jerusalem, Luke emphasizes the essential continuity between the church in Jerusalem and the mission of Paul to the nations. After being welcomed warmly by the elders of the mother church, Paul recounts the details of his work among the Gentiles and how God blessed his mission (vv. 17–19). The leaders in Jerusalem praise God for the response of the Gentiles to the gospel, acknowledging that this is truly God's work (v. 20).

Not only has the mission to the Gentiles borne fruit, but Jerusalem's mission to the Jews has also been a success. Among them there are "many thousands of believers" (v. 20). Yet, among these Jewish Christians there has arisen much misunderstanding of Paul's mission and hostility toward him. Because these Jewish believers are zealous not only about Jesus the Messiah but also about the law of Moses, they question Paul's own fidelity to his Jewish heritage. They had been told that Paul taught the Jews living among the Gentiles to forsake Moses, telling them not to circumcise their sons or practice the traditions of Israel (v. 21). Thus, the elders urge Paul to demonstrate his loyalty to Judaism by sponsoring four men in the traditional Nazirite ritual (Num. 6:1–21). Paul accompanies them in their purification and brings them into the temple in an attempt to appease his opponents.

Paul, like Jesus, had been falsely accused. He had always remained loyal to the Torah and the faith of Israel, even when working among the Gentiles. There is never any indication in Acts or in Paul's letters that he advocated Jewish believers forsaking the practices of the Torah. Paul's return from his missionary travels to the mother church in Jerusalem shows the essential unity of the church's mission both to the Jews and to the Gentiles. This unity in Christ, between Jewish and Gentile believers, demonstrates that while the church must always reach outside itself, it must always return to its apostolic roots for approval and guidance. Paul finds his motivation for his missionary work within the tradition itself.

Consider this question based on your lectio of the Scripture and commentary:

✞ What is the reason for the unusual gestures of the prophet Agabus? Why did he choose to act out his prophecy?

Meditatio

Take some time to ponder whatever words and phrases from the reading struck you. Reflect on these questions in that spirit of meditation.

✝ What are some of the echoes from the passion of Jesus in this passage about Paul? What does this say about Paul's motivations?

✝ Paul firmly believes that God's covenant with Israel is the source of God's blessing to all the nations. How is Paul's mission to the Gentiles rooted in tradition? In what ways was Paul's mission misunderstood by the Jewish members of the church in Jerusalem?

✝ What does the return of Paul, the missionary to the Gentiles, to the church in Jerusalem indicate to me about the apostolic and universal qualities of the church?

Oratio

Speak to God in response to the words, ideas, and images of your reflective reading.

> God of all nations, you called Paul, the apostle to the Gentiles, to return to the church of the Jews in Jerusalem. Help your church to understand its Jewish roots and the tradition of Israel in which it stands. Help me to realize that the church of Jesus is one, holy, catholic, and apostolic.

Continue to pray in union with Christ's church in whatever words you wish . . .

Contemplatio

As you rest in the peace that God gives to those who seek it, slowly repeat the phrase "the Lord's will be done" (v. 14). Allow God to give you confidence as you trust in him.

After a period of quiet contemplation, write a few words about your experience.

Operatio

Paul was confident in living out God's will through his mission and sought God's will for each new move. Ask God to reveal his will for you in this moment. Act upon your understanding of God's desire for your life today.

12

The Faithful Jew Sent
to the Gentiles

Lectio

*Read this passage aloud so that you will experience the Scripture more fully
by seeing it with your eyes, hearing it with your ears, and speaking it with
your lips.*

ACTS 21:40–22:21

40When [the tribune] had given him permission, Paul stood on the
steps and motioned to the people for silence; and when there was a
great hush, he addressed them in the Hebrew language, saying:

1"Brothers and fathers, listen to the defense that I now make before you."

2When they heard him addressing them in Hebrew, they became
even more quiet. Then he said:

3"I am a Jew, born in Tarsus in Cilicia, but brought up in this city
at the feet of Gamaliel, educated strictly according to our ancestral
law, being zealous for God, just as all of you are today. 4I persecuted
this Way up to the point of death by binding both men and women
and putting them in prison, 5as the high priest and the whole council
of elders can testify about me. From them I also received letters to the
brothers in Damascus, and I went there in order to bind those who
were there and to bring them back to Jerusalem for punishment.

⁶"While I was on my way and approaching Damascus, about noon a great light from heaven suddenly shone about me. ⁷I fell to the ground and heard a voice saying to me, 'Saul, Saul, why are you persecuting me?' ⁸I answered, 'Who are you, Lord?' Then he said to me, 'I am Jesus of Nazareth whom you are persecuting.' ⁹Now those who were with me saw the light but did not hear the voice of the one who was speaking to me. ¹⁰I asked, 'What am I to do, Lord?' The Lord said to me, 'Get up and go to Damascus; there you will be told everything that has been assigned to you to do.' ¹¹Since I could not see because of the brightness of that light, those who were with me took my hand and led me to Damascus.

¹²"A certain Ananias, who was a devout man according to the law and well spoken of by all the Jews living there, ¹³came to me; and standing beside me, he said, 'Brother Saul, regain your sight!' In that very hour I regained my sight and saw him. ¹⁴Then he said, 'The God of our ancestors has chosen you to know his will, to see the Righteous One and to hear his own voice; ¹⁵for you will be his witness to all the world of what you have seen and heard. ¹⁶And now why do you delay? Get up, be baptized, and have your sins washed away, calling on his name.'

¹⁷"After I had returned to Jerusalem and while I was praying in the temple, I fell into a trance ¹⁸and saw Jesus saying to me, 'Hurry and get out of Jerusalem quickly, because they will not accept your testimony about me.' ¹⁹And I said, 'Lord, they themselves know that in every synagogue I imprisoned and beat those who believed in you. ²⁰And while the blood of your witness Stephen was shed, I myself was standing by, approving and keeping the coats of those who killed him.' ²¹Then he said to me, 'Go, for I will send you far away to the Gentiles.'"

After dwelling with this Scripture, continue to develop your understanding of the text with the following commentary:

Paul is given permission by the Roman tribune to speak to the crowd in Jerusalem who seeks his death. From the steps of the temple, Paul motions with his hands like an orator and begins his speech in his own defense. He is a Jew speaking to his fellow Jews. In an attempt to win their goodwill, he speaks in the Hebrew language, the Aramaic of Palestine. The crowd grows profoundly silent and listens intently. The speech falls into three parts. First,

Paul recounts his earlier life in Judaism (vv. 3–5); second, he speaks about the event along the road to Damascus (vv. 6–11); and third, he recalls his divine commission to be the apostle to the Gentiles (vv. 12–21).

Paul proudly states, "I am a Jew" (v. 3). Though born in Tarsus, he was raised in Jerusalem and taught the written and oral tradition of Judaism at the feet of the great rabbi Gamaliel. Zealous for God, Paul was educated strictly in the law of Israel. In language, upbringing, and zealotry, he was like his audience. To the Jewish Christians, he had appeared as a persecutor of the church, arresting believers and casting them into prison (v. 4). Thus far, Paul was a devout Jewish Pharisee with unequaled credentials.

Next, Paul recounts the transforming events that happened to him along the road to Damascus. Though it was noon, when the sun would be most intense, Paul was blinded by a greater light, the glory of God's presence. The voice of the risen Lord told him to go to Damascus, where he would be told what to do.

The instrument of Paul's divine commission was Ananias, a devout Jewish man in Damascus. In delivering the words of Paul's calling, Ananias told Paul that the God of Israel's past had chosen him to be a witness to the will of God in the present, to proclaim to the world what he had seen and heard, the divine glory and the voice of the risen Lord. Paul's commission was subsequently confirmed by a vision as he was praying in the temple (v. 17), a calling resembling the prophetic call of Isaiah, who had a vision of the Lord in the temple (Isa. 6:1–10). Here Paul saw a vision of the Lord, who commanded him to leave Jerusalem and to go "far away to the Gentiles" (v. 21).

Paul's intention in recounting all this to the crowd was to show that his work among the Gentiles was not his own choice but that of the Lord. Though he wished to stay in Jerusalem, the Lord sent him away to the Gentiles. He did not forsake Judaism. Rather, the God of Judaism called him to go to the nations, to be a light of deliverance so that their eyes too could be opened to the presence of God among them.

Respond to this question based on your lectio of the Scripture and commentary:

‡ Why did Paul want to address the crowd and recount the events of his life to them? Which similarities between Paul and the crowd did he choose to emphasize in this speech?

Meditatio

Consider the ways God has worked within your own life. Reflect on the words of Paul's speech in light of your experience of God's guidance.

‡ Paul describes God's transforming work in his life in three stages. Which three moments of my life would I describe in explaining to others the way God has directed me?

‡ What are some of the ways God prepared Paul from his early life for his divinely given commission? What unique circumstances have prepared me for my Christian mission?

‡ Paul thought he would be an ideal evangelist to the Jews of Jerusalem, but the risen Lord sent him away to the Gentiles. How has God redirected my life in a way I did not expect?

Oratio

Speak to God in response to the words, ideas, and images of your reflective reading.

> God of our ancestors, you called Paul to be your instrument for your new work in the world. Keep me rooted in the past but always open to the new ways you are guiding your church. Prepare me each day to be your instrument in the world.

Use your own words to continue your prayer . . .

Contemplatio

When words are no longer useful, just rest in the light of the risen Lord, who calls you and directs your life in ways that go beyond your expectations.

After a period of quiet contemplation, write a few words about your experience.

Operatio

God is directing my life in conformity with his plan for the future. What is one action I could take in the coming days to respond to God's direction for my life?

13

Paul's First Letter Expresses Joyful Thanksgiving

Lectio

Read the Scripture as you would read an eagerly anticipated letter.

1 THESSALONIANS 1:1–2:8

[1]Paul, Silvanus, and Timothy, To the church of the Thessalonians in God the Father and the Lord Jesus Christ:

Grace to you and peace.

[2]We always give thanks to God for all of you and mention you in our prayers, constantly [3]remembering before our God and Father your work of faith and labor of love and steadfastness of hope in our Lord Jesus Christ. [4]For we know, brothers and sisters beloved by God, that he has chosen you, [5]because our message of the gospel came to you not in word only, but also in power and in the Holy Spirit and with full conviction; just as you know what kind of persons we proved to be among you for your sake. [6]And you became imitators of us and of the Lord, for in spite of persecution you received the word with joy inspired by the Holy Spirit, [7]so that you became an example to all the believers in Macedonia and in Achaia. [8]For the word of the Lord has sounded forth from you not only in Macedonia and Achaia, but

in every place your faith in God has become known, so that we have no need to speak about it. ⁹For the people of those regions report about us what kind of welcome we had among you, and how you turned to God from idols, to serve a living and true God, ¹⁰and to wait for his Son from heaven, whom he raised from the dead—Jesus, who rescues us from the wrath that is coming.

¹You yourselves know, brothers and sisters, that our coming to you was not in vain, ²but though we had already suffered and been shamefully mistreated at Philippi, as you know, we had courage in our God to declare to you the gospel of God in spite of great opposition. ³For our appeal does not spring from deceit or impure motives or trickery, ⁴but just as we have been approved by God to be entrusted with the message of the gospel, even so we speak, not to please mortals, but to please God who tests our hearts. ⁵As you know and as God is our witness, we never came with words of flattery or with a pretext for greed; ⁶nor did we seek praise from mortals, whether from you or from others, ⁷though we might have made demands as apostles of Christ. But we were gentle among you, like a nurse tenderly caring for her own children. ⁸So deeply do we care for you that we are determined to share with you not only the gospel of God but also our own selves, because you have become very dear to us.

After taking the words of Paul's letter to heart, continue to search for the message within his words.

This letter is generally regarded by scholars as the first existing writing from Paul. Written in the middle of the first century, it is the earliest Christian writing and, thus, the earliest evidence of Christianity. The salutation follows the pattern for letters of that time: the authors are named, the recipients are listed, and then the recipients are greeted formally. Silvanus and Timothy are Paul's travel companions, working with him to establish "the church of the Thessalonians." Paul is never a solo performer; he always evangelizes as part of a collaborative team. The "church" in Thessalonica refers to the gathering of Christians there and consists of one or more house churches. Paul's unique greeting, "grace to you and peace" (1:1), carries us to the heart of the gospel, for we are saved by the grace of God that we might have peace with God.

Paul's letters generally follow the address and greeting with words of thanksgiving for his readers. In this letter, he states that whenever he and his companions pray, they always give thanks to God for the Thessalonian church. They particularly remember with gratitude three things: their "work of faith," their "labor of love," and their "steadfastness of hope" (1:3). This familiar triad of graces (faith, love, and hope) effectively sums up Paul's vision of the Christian life and describes the life of the community in Thessalonica.

Paul and his companions bring the "message of the gospel" to the community, yet that message cannot be effectively communicated unless it is proclaimed "in power and in the Holy Spirit and with full conviction" (1:5). God's power through the Holy Spirit affects both the bringer and the receiver of the gospel. The full conviction of the preacher is rooted in divine power, and it is this same Spirit who convinces the hearer of the truth of the gospel they have received. The work of proclaiming and hearing the gospel is a wonderful fusion of divine and human elements. This incarnate gospel is received "with joy inspired by the Holy Spirit" despite persecution or any other obstacle (1:6).

The church in Thessalonica has been widely praised throughout the region, and their reception of the gospel has become a means of evangelizing others (1:7–8). Paul uses three verbs to describe their inspiring response, turn, serve, and wait (1:9–10), which correspond to the previously mentioned virtues of faith, love, and hope. They "turned to God from idols," changing their hearts and putting away all the idols that impeded their faith in God. This conversion implies two further responses: "to serve a living and true God" and "to wait for his Son from heaven." This serving and waiting complement one another. There is no other way to wait for God than to serve God here and now, and the service of love is motivated by the confident hope in which we wait.

In the first chapter of the letter, Paul focuses on the experience of the Thessalonians. In the second, he highlights his own work among them. Paul and his companions have been "entrusted with the message of the gospel" (2:4). Despite suffering and opposition, they spoke with courage and avoided the vices of which they were accused by their detractors: deception, trickery, flattery, greed, and praise. So like a mother nursing her own children, they cared for the community and shared with them not only the gospel but also their very selves (2:7–8).

Meditatio

Reflect on how the inspired text speaks God's Word to the circumstances of your own life.

‡ In what way does the life of the Thessalonian community inspire others and attract them to the gospel? In what ways is my Christian community an evangelizer of others by the way we live?

‡ What primary characteristics of a minister of the gospel are highlighted in this letter? Which of these do I want to develop in myself?

‡ What characteristics have you noticed in Christian ministers that most repel you from the Good News of Christ? How can you and your community avoid these negative characteristics in your own life of faith?

Oratio

Speak to God, like Paul, in thanksgiving for the ways you have been influenced by the gospel and its ministers.

I thank you, God, for the preaching and writing of Paul and for the way he has brought the gospel to others. I thank you for the people and events of my life that have helped me to understand your Word and to live in Christ.

Continue to pray to God with gratitude for the ways the Good News has been shown to you . . .

Contemplatio

Remain in wordless silence, grateful to God for the gifts of faith, love, and hope. Ask God to increase these graces within you.

Write a few words about your experience of God in silence.

Operatio

Decide today how you want to change your life to better reflect your faith and convictions. Choose one way of demonstrating your faith in love.

14

Waiting in Hope for the Coming of the Lord

Lectio

In a comfortable and quiet place, read the Scripture carefully, asking God's Spirit to guide you in your understanding.

1 THESSALONIANS 4:13–5:11

[13]But we do not want you to be uninformed, brothers and sisters, about those who have died, so that you may not grieve as others do who have no hope. [14]For since we believe that Jesus died and rose again, even so, through Jesus, God will bring with him those who have died. [15]For this we declare to you by the word of the Lord, that we who are alive, who are left until the coming of the Lord, will by no means precede those who have died. [16]For the Lord himself, with a cry of command, with the archangel's call and with the sound of God's trumpet, will descend from heaven, and the dead in Christ will rise first. [17]Then we who are alive, who are left, will be caught up in the clouds together with them to meet the Lord in the air; and so we will be with the Lord forever. [18]Therefore encourage one another with these words.

[1]Now concerning the times and the seasons, brothers and sisters, you do not need to have anything written to you. [2]For you yourselves know

very well that the day of the Lord will come like a thief in the night. [3]When they say, "There is peace and security," then sudden destruction will come upon them, as labor pains come upon a pregnant woman, and there will be no escape! [4]But you, beloved, are not in darkness, for that day to surprise you like a thief; [5]for you are all children of light and children of the day; we are not of the night or of darkness. [6]So then let us not fall asleep as others do, but let us keep awake and be sober; [7]for those who sleep sleep at night, and those who are drunk get drunk at night. [8]But since we belong to the day, let us be sober, and put on the breastplate of faith and love, and for a helmet the hope of salvation. [9]For God has destined us not for wrath but for obtaining salvation through our Lord Jesus Christ, [10]who died for us, so that whether we are awake or asleep we may live with him.

[11]Therefore encourage one another and build up each other, as indeed you are doing.

After allowing Paul's words to sink into your mind and heart, continue to listen for Paul's meaning through these remarks:

Hope in God and waiting for the coming of Jesus Christ are the principal themes of Paul's letter. Here Paul writes as a pastor in two closely connected sections: first, he addresses the issue of hope for believers who have already died within the community (4:13–18), and second, he speaks about the character of Christian waiting for the Lord's coming (5:1–11). Each section concludes with the assurance that we will always be with the Lord (4:17; 5:10) and with the exhortation that we should "encourage one another" (4:18; 5:11).

Paul first responds to the grief felt within the community for those who have died. Paul is not discouraging the expression of grief; rather, he states that the grief of Christians is different from the grief of those "who have no hope" (4:13). He offers them assurance and a reason for their hope. Those who believe that Christ died and that he rose also believe that he will come again (4:14). But this faith is intimately connected with our own dying and rising. Those who have died in Christ will also rise again from death and will participate in God's final triumph when Jesus returns.

The early Christians had a vivid expectation that the coming of Jesus would be very soon, probably within the lifetime of many. This sense of waiting with anticipation is an attitude that Paul's writings continue to instill within the church in every age. The images of trumpet blasts, the call of angels, and Christ's descent on the clouds are images common in both Jewish and Christian final-age literature at the time (4:16). Paul's imagery primarily serves to assure the community that Christ will come again to reign and that they will be with him forever. In the assurance of Christ's future coming, God gives us hope that we will finally prevail over death. This is the difference between the grief of Christians and that of those without hope.

Paul's second section teaches us that while Christ's coming can be trusted, it cannot be predicted (5:1). We must have confidence and hope, but we cannot name the day or control the circumstances. Paul uses the familiar New Testament images of the thief that breaks into the house and the labor pains of pregnancy to describe the unexpected suddenness and inevitability of "the day of the Lord" (5:2–3). While the images are frightening, Paul states that the sudden terror has no power over those who are in Christ. We are "children of light and children of the day" (5:5), so there is no need to fear the darkness in which the thief operates or to be surprised by the terrors that lurk in the night. Paul finally urges us to live according to our calling in Christ. Since we belong to the day and the light, we should remain awake, sober, and watchful (5:6–7), not consumed with anxiety but confident, encouraging one another in the salvation promised us.

After reading Paul's pastoral response to this community's anxiety, write your response to these questions:

1 ‡ What encouragement does Paul offer to those who grieve for the dead?

2 ‡ Why does Paul distinguish between trusting in Christ's coming and predicting it?

Meditatio

After reflecting on this section of Paul's letter, ask yourself how the text expands your relationship with God.

‡ Why does Paul put the ministry of consolation in the hands of the community? As a Christian, how can I help people to grieve with hope?

‡ What is the essence of Paul's description of Christ's coming again? In what ways can this Christian belief help to relieve people of anxieties and fears?

‡ Why does Paul describe faith, love, and hope as the armor of a Christian (5:8)? How does such armor protect me and give me confidence?

Oratio

Remember that whether we are awake or asleep, we are with the Lord. Pray to God who is always present and faithful to you.

> Faithful Lord, I believe that Christ died and rose and that he will come again in glory. Help me to trust in your promises and help me to grieve the death of my loved ones as one who has hope in the resurrection and in the life of the world to come.

Continue praying to the God of life in words that arise from within the fears and confidence of your heart . . .

Contemplatio

Place yourself in the embrace of God, who wants only life and salvation for you. Allow God's desires for you to dissolve your anxieties about the future.

Write a few words describing your contemplative experience of God's care.

Operatio

Paul urges us to encourage and build up one another with his words. Which words of Paul could I use to support those who need greater hope?

15

Chosen as the First Fruits for Salvation

Lectio

Close off the distractions of the day and enter a still moment. Read this text aloud so that you hear the words and listen to the inspired message.

2 THESSALONIANS 2:13–3:5

[13]But we must always give thanks to God for you, brothers and sisters beloved by the Lord, because God chose you as the first fruits for salvation through sanctification by the Spirit and through belief in the truth. [14]For this purpose he called you through our proclamation of the good news, so that you may obtain the glory of our Lord Jesus Christ. [15]So then, brothers and sisters, stand firm and hold fast to the traditions that you were taught by us, either by word of mouth or by our letter.

[16]Now may our Lord Jesus Christ himself and God our Father, who loved us and through grace gave us eternal comfort and good hope, [17]comfort your hearts and strengthen them in every good work and word.

[1]Finally, brothers and sisters, pray for us, so that the word of the Lord may spread rapidly and be glorified everywhere, just as it is among you, [2]and that we may be rescued from wicked and evil people;

for not all have faith. ³But the Lord is faithful; he will strengthen you and guard you from the evil one. ⁴And we have confidence in the Lord concerning you, that you are doing and will go on doing the things that we command. ⁵May the Lord direct your hearts to the love of God and to the steadfastness of Christ.

Having listened to God's Word, continue to search for the meaning and message through these comments:

Paul addresses the church at Thessalonica as "brothers and sisters beloved by the Lord" (2:13). The brothers and sisters are those whose new birth has made them children of God the Father and one family in him. Not only are they loved by Paul and one another, but they are also first beloved of God and loved by Christ as members of his family. This love of God, which is the source of their salvation in Christ, continues to enfold them despite the sufferings and challenges of their calling.

Paul gives thanks to God for the community because God "chose" them "for salvation" (2:13). As always in his writing, Paul places a strong emphasis on God's initiative. God's choice is made not on the basis of human merit but according to God's eternal plan and his saving purposes for humanity. They were chosen as God's "first fruits" (2:13), a term that indicates an early harvest of which there is more to come. The Thessalonians are only the beginning; the full harvest of evangelization that God intends has yet to be gathered.

The term "salvation" embraces the whole work of God in Christ on our behalf. Its implications for believers and for the world are past, present, and future. The means by which we experience this salvation in the present are "through sanctification by the Spirit," God's work on our behalf, and "through belief in the truth," our human response in faith (2:13). This weighty verse summarizes the internal process by which we become Christians. First, we are chosen through God's grace. Next, the Holy Spirit makes effective within our hearts the work of Christ. Finally, we respond in faith, welcoming Christ's work within us and inviting God's Spirit to act within us.

Not only has God chosen us, but he has also "called" us. This divine calling comes through the "proclamation of the good news" (2:14). The preaching of the gospel by Paul and his companions first made the Thessalonians aware of God's call. The ultimate purpose of God's call is that we might "obtain the glory of our Lord Jesus Christ" (2:14). That glory was manifested in part at the coming of Christ to the world and is experienced by believers in the Christian life. But the complete manifestation of Christ's glory will be made at his return. Our full sharing in that glory will make our salvation complete.

Since God loves us, has chosen us, and has called us, Paul urges us to "stand firm and hold fast to the traditions" (2:15). "Traditions" refer here to the authoritative beliefs and practices that have been handed on to the community through the preaching and teaching of the apostles. Paul notes that these traditions have been taught both "by word of mouth" and "by our letter" (2:15). In urging the church to stand firm and hold fast to these traditions, he wants the community to understand that these teachings form the sure apostolic foundation through which they can resist false teachings and discern the will of God in the challenges of their life ahead.

Paul's thanksgiving turns to petition, asking God the Father and Jesus Christ to comfort and strengthen us (2:16–17). Again Paul emphasizes God's work within us, giving us the ability to produce "every good work and word" (2:17). What we are by God's grace is what we should increasingly manifest in our Christian behavior, through both good works and good words.

After you have listened for the Word of the Lord, answer these questions:

‡ What does this passage say about the how and why of God's salvation?

‡ For what does Paul ask the community to pray as he concludes his letter to them?

Meditatio

Read the first three verses of Paul's words again, listening for God's personal Word to you. Pause to meditate each time a phrase speaks to you.

‡ What is the specific reason Christians may call themselves brothers and sisters? What are the implications of using these terms to address others?

‡ How does Paul describe the process by which we become Christians? In what way is this process a combination of both divine and human movements?

‡ In what ways has God called me, as Paul describes, through the proclamation of the gospel? How have I responded?

Oratio

Let Paul's words teach you how to pray. Read 2 Thessalonians 2:16–17 as a model prayer.

> God our Father and our Lord Jesus Christ, I praise you for the love and grace you have shown to me. Encourage me and give me strength for the challenges I face. May my words and deeds always show others the source of the hope I have in you.

Continue voicing the prayer that issues from your heart . . .

Contemplatio

Rest in the trusting and confident faith God has given you. Be assured that God is at work within you through his grace.

Write a few words about your time of contemplatio.

Operatio

I want to be more aware today that God is leading me to a fuller "sanctification by the Spirit" and "belief in the truth" (2:13). What could I do to cooperate more with God's grace?

16

It Is Christ
Who Lives in Me

Lectio

Read Paul's famous text on justification with new eyes. Allow yourself to come to a renewed understanding of Christian faith.

GALATIANS 2:15–21

[15]We ourselves are Jews by birth and not Gentile sinners; [16]yet we know that a person is justified not by the works of the law but through faith in Jesus Christ. And we have come to believe in Christ Jesus, so that we might be justified by faith in Christ, and not by doing the works of the law, because no one will be justified by the works of the law. [17]But if, in our effort to be justified in Christ, we ourselves have been found to be sinners, is Christ then a servant of sin? Certainly not! [18]But if I build up again the very things that I once tore down, then I demonstrate that I am a transgressor. [19]For through the law I died to the law, so that I might live to God. I have been crucified with Christ; [20]and it is no longer I who live, but it is Christ who lives in me. And the life I now live in the flesh I live by faith in the Son of God, who loved me and gave himself for me. [21]I do not nullify the grace of God; for if justification comes through the law, then Christ died for nothing.

Having heard God's Word through the words of his apostle Paul, continue to explore the church's understanding of these words.

As a person born into Judaism, Paul had previously assumed that the primary division within humanity is that of Jew and Gentile (v. 15). He took for granted that Jews stand within the covenant, and by obeying the precepts of the Torah, they lead righteous lives and walk blamelessly before God. By contrast, the Gentiles stand outside the covenant, deprived of the blessings of the Torah, and are therefore sinners. Yet, Paul's traditional understanding of God's will for humanity had been radically transformed when he encountered the risen Christ.

Paul's ministry to bring the gospel to the Gentiles was threatened in Galatia by a group of rival teachers who were insisting that circumcision and the practice of Jewish dietary laws were essential for Gentile believers in Christ. Paul and his fellow evangelizers proclaimed, in contrast, that the essence of Christianity is living in Jesus Christ through faith. This meant that Gentiles are included in the Christian community on no different level or no different terms than Jews.

Paul and his companions came to realize that no one can be "justified by the works of the law" (v. 16). The term "justified" comes from the language of the law courts, in which it means "to be found in the right, to be acquitted." It is the verdict one would want to hear if one were on trial. Being justified, in the context of Paul's understanding, means being acquitted by God, being freed from the guilt of sin, being made right with God. This divine acquittal results in a new life for the believer. "The works of the law" refer to circumcision, following dietary laws, keeping the Sabbath, and obeying other ordinances contained in the Torah that distinguish Jews from Gentiles. Paul came to understand that the outward signs of being a Jew, as important as these things are to the Jewish tradition, are not sufficient to place anyone in a right relationship with God. In fact, neither a Jew nor a Gentile could be justified on the basis of performing these legal works.

Paul teaches that justification is a grace from God, a divine gift that cannot be merited or earned by its receiver. Justification comes not through legal works but through faith. Most versions of the Bible translate this phrase as "through faith in Jesus Christ" (v. 16). However, an increasing number of scholars translate this important teaching as "through the faith of Jesus Christ." The emphasis is placed not on what believers do but on what Christ has done. Believers are justified before God through Christ's faith, the faith Jesus showed through his trust in the Father's will, his obedience that led to the cross, and his faithfulness in carrying out the mission entrusted to him.

Paul has set up a vivid contrast between "the works of the law" (v. 16) and "the faith of Christ." If a work of the law, like dietary regulations, is demanded of Gentiles to ensure their inclusion in God's people, then what is the point of Christ's death? If Christians put their trust in the law, they thereby reject the work of Christ, for "if justification comes through the law, then Christ died for nothing" (v. 21). Gentiles do not need to be circumcised, follow dietary laws, and observe the Sabbath rules to become members of God's people in Christ. If Paul were to "build up again" the necessity of the law, he would be a "transgressor" of the gospel, for he has "died to the law" in order to live for God in Jesus Christ (vv. 18–19).

For Paul, the heart of the Christian life is conformity to Jesus Christ, living in him. Paul describes the essence of this new life: "It is no longer I who live, but it is Christ who lives in me" (v. 20). By being "crucified with Christ" (v. 19), the Christian is incorporated into Christ and lives "in Christ." Justification, then, is sharing the faith of Christ, participating in Christ's relationship with the Father, membership of Jews and Gentiles together in the one family of God.

After listening for the meaning of this sacred text, answer these questions:

✝ What is Paul's understanding of justification? How does Paul teach that justification is accomplished?

✝ Why is trusting in the works of the law a denial of the effectiveness of Christ's death?

Meditatio

Spend some time reflecting on the implications of Paul's teaching for you.

‡ Scholars offer two alternative translations of Paul's words: "I live by faith in the Son of God" and "I live by the faith of the Son of God" (v. 20). What is the difference between these two alternatives for understanding the Christian life?

‡ What is the heart of the Christian life, according to Paul's teachings? How do I understand this in practical terms for my own life?

‡ Paul expresses reverence for the law in this letter, and in another letter, he says, "The law is holy" (Rom. 7:12). How can I demonstrate respect for the law and also reject the necessity of following the precepts of the law for those who are in Christ?

Oratio

Since Christ lives in you, allow the Spirit of Christ to pray within your heart.

God of Jews and Gentiles, you desire to form one people in your Son, Jesus. Though we had done nothing to deserve salvation, Jesus loved us and gave himself for us. Help me to realize that I cannot earn your forgiveness and life with you but that you have freely given it to me through the faith of Jesus Christ.

Continue praying to God, using the thoughts and words of Paul's text...

Contemplatio

Slowly repeat the words, "It is no longer I who live, but it is Christ who lives in me." Allow these words to slowly penetrate your entire being as you remain in contemplative silence.

Write a few words summarizing your contemplative experience of being "in Christ."

Operatio

After contemplatively seeking to open your life to the indwelling of Christ, consider the implications of living that contemplative experience in an active way. Become an active contemplative and a contemplative activist. To what is Christ calling me?

17

Promised Heirs
of the Father

Lectio

Continue slowly reading Paul's teachings to the Galatians, seeking to understand the meaning and implications of life in Christ.

GALATIANS 3:23–4:7

[23]Now before faith came, we were imprisoned and guarded under the law until faith would be revealed. [24]Therefore the law was our disciplinarian until Christ came, so that we might be justified by faith. [25]But now that faith has come, we are no longer subject to a disciplinarian, [26]for in Christ Jesus you are all children of God through faith. [27]As many of you as were baptized into Christ have clothed yourselves with Christ. [28]There is no longer Jew or Greek, there is no longer slave or free, there is no longer male and female; for all of you are one in Christ Jesus. [29]And if you belong to Christ, then you are Abraham's offspring, heirs according to the promise.

[1]My point is this: heirs, as long as they are minors, are no better than slaves, though they are the owners of all the property; [2]but they remain under guardians and trustees until the date set by the father. [3]So with us; while we were minors, we were enslaved to the elemental

spirits of the world. ⁴But when the fullness of time had come, God sent his Son, born of a woman, born under the law, ⁵in order to redeem those who were under the law, so that we might receive adoption as children. ⁶And because you are children, God has sent the Spirit of his Son into our hearts, crying, "Abba! Father!" ⁷So you are no longer a slave but a child, and if a child then also an heir, through God.

As you continue to listen for God's Word through Paul's letter, search now for fuller meaning through the teaching and scholarship of the church.

Paul demonstrates that the law had a significant role in the promises of God and his saving plan. Before the coming of faith, the law served as a "disciplinarian" (3:24–25). Paul draws on the image of the Greek *paidagogos*, a slave within the household who served as a guardian and guide for the children. The role of this servant was to safeguard and protect the youths, confining their freedom, until they came of age. In using this image, Paul teaches that before the coming of Christ, the law served as a custodian for God's people. Its protective and confining role was time limited, from the time of Moses to the appearance of Jesus Christ.

"Now that faith has come" refers to the coming of Christ. The manifestation of his faith—his trust in God's plan and his obedience in life and in death—marks the time of fulfillment for God's people. The work of Christ manifested the limitations of the law and its inability to justify and save sinners. The law could tell people they were transgressing God's will, but it did not give them the power to follow God's will. Only when living in the faith of Christ and following his Spirit can people truly live as God desires.

The Torah, or law of Israel, has not lost its value for Christians. Its moral precepts are valuable guides for those seeking to follow God's will. Jesus is the culmination of the Torah, which includes Moses, the giving of the law at Sinai, and the establishment of Israel's worship. The Torah lays the foundation, provides the context, and gives meaning to the Christian gospel. To neglect the Torah is to deprive Christ of his Jewish roots. "Born of a woman, born under the law" (4:4), the Jewish Messiah brought the Torah to the whole world.

Paul tells his Gentile readers that they are "children of God through faith" (3:26). The designation "children of God" was the privilege of Israel due to God's choice and calling. But because believers are now "in Christ" through faith, both Gentiles and Jews are "Abraham's offspring" and heirs of God's promises (3:29). All believers are now children of God because they have been "baptized into Christ" and have "clothed" themselves with Christ (3:27). In baptism, Christ envelops the believer like a garment, and the believer begins to live as a new creation in Christ. The racial, social, and sexual differences that painfully divide people in the world have no relevance for those baptized into Christ (3:28). This new identity, rooted in and defined by Christ, transcends the barriers erected by human society. One who has this new identity can truly be called a new creation.

As Paul continues to explain the relationship between the law and faith, he offers another image. The heirs of an estate are unable to inherit their property while they are still minors. Even though they technically own the estate, they must remain subject to guardians and trustees until the time appointed by the father for them to take charge of the property (4:1–2). Paul says that the condition of those who maintain the law as their identity is like the situation of heirs to the estate who are still minors. They were given the promises of the covenant, but the fullness of their inheritance awaited the date set by the Father. During this period, the Jews were confined by the legal works that separated them from the Gentile world, and the Gentiles were enslaved to the "elemental spirits" of false gods and a life determined by fate and the forces of the cosmos (4:3).

But when the time set by the Father arrived, God graciously sent his Son "to redeem those . . . under the law" so that all might "receive adoption as children" (4:4–5). As adopted children, we have been called into God's family through no merit of our own and given the inheritance promised to us. As God's children, we have received the Spirit of his Son into our hearts, enabling us to call out "Abba! Father!" (4:6) just as Jesus did.

After carefully reading the Scripture and commentary, answer this question:

‡ In what way does Paul describe the precepts of the law as part of God's saving plan for the Jewish people?

Meditatio

Spend some time reflecting on the text, asking yourself what personal message the passage has for you.

‡ If the Torah has no power to save us, why is it so important for Christians to read and understand it? How much time have I spent studying the first five books of the Bible?

‡ What are some barriers that divide groups of people from one another today? How does the gospel Paul preached challenge these boundaries and hostilities between people?

‡ I am an orphan who has been graciously adopted by God to share in the life of his family. How does this realization help me to call out "Abba! Father!" with deeper meaning and purpose?

Oratio

Realizing that God has adopted you and given you an eternal inheritance, pray to God with a grateful heart.

Abba, Father, you have called me out of a world of slavery and confusion, and you have adopted me into your family. Give me an awareness of the inheritance you have promised me, and give me a spirit of thankfulness to praise you. Send your Spirit into my heart to make me a grateful and joyful child of your kingdom.

Continue responding to God with words generated by your reflection on the Scripture . . .

Contemplatio

Imagine yourself embraced by God, your loving Father. If this is a comfortable image for you, rest in his arms, call out "Abba," and let your heart be filled with gratitude for his goodness and love.

Write a brief note about experiencing God as Abba.

Operatio

If people are joined into the unity of Christ in baptism and called to share in the one family of God, what can I do to break down the national, ethnic, racial, sexual, and cultural barriers that divide people and promote misunderstanding and hostility?

18

The Fruit of the
Holy Spirit

Lectio

Ask the Holy Spirit to guide your reading as the Word of God reshapes your ideas about the life you are called to live.

GALATIANS 5:13–26

¹³For you were called to freedom, brothers and sisters; only do not use your freedom as an opportunity for self-indulgence, but through love become slaves to one another. ¹⁴For the whole law is summed up in a single commandment, "You shall love your neighbor as yourself." ¹⁵If, however, you bite and devour one another, take care that you are not consumed by one another.

¹⁶Live by the Spirit, I say, and do not gratify the desires of the flesh. ¹⁷For what the flesh desires is opposed to the Spirit, and what the Spirit desires is opposed to the flesh; for these are opposed to each other, to prevent you from doing what you want. ¹⁸But if you are led by the Spirit, you are not subject to the law. ¹⁹Now the works of the flesh are obvious: fornication, impurity, licentiousness, ²⁰idolatry, sorcery, enmities, strife, jealousy, anger, quarrels, dissensions, factions, ²¹envy, drunkenness, carousing, and things like these. I am warning you, as

I warned you before: those who do such things will not inherit the kingdom of God.

²²By contrast, the fruit of the Spirit is love, joy, peace, patience, kindness, generosity, faithfulness, ²³gentleness, and self-control. There is no law against such things. ²⁴And those who belong to Christ Jesus have crucified the flesh with its passions and desires. ²⁵If we live by the Spirit, let us also be guided by the Spirit. ²⁶Let us not become conceited, competing against one another, envying one another.

Continue your search for the significance of Paul's writing by listening to the voice of the church's teaching.

Paul teaches that one of the primary characteristics of the Christian life is freedom. He warns his readers not to abuse their God-given freedom and offers advice for living a free life in Christ. Just as their Hebrew ancestors had to learn in the wilderness how to live as a free people after being liberated from the bondage of Egypt, these new Christians must learn how to live their new life in freedom. They must not mistake their new freedom for permissive self-indulgence, which ironically becomes a kind of slavery (v. 13). Rather, the way of gospel freedom is a movement beyond comfort and security to the risks of love and the challenges of service. Paul charges his listeners: "Through love become slaves to one another" (v. 13). Paradoxically, this kind of enslavement is the best way to preserve one's freedom.

Unlike contemporary thought in which freedom is understood as a life without restraints, Paul has no trouble speaking about law in the same context as freedom. Following a commandment is the way to grow in freedom, especially that precept that summarizes the whole law: "You shall love your neighbor as yourself" (v. 14). Originating in the Torah (Lev. 19:18) and taught by Jesus (Matt. 22:39), the command to love is rooted in the love God has for us and the example of Jesus's love unto death. Those who have been set free by Jesus are given the vocation to love one another.

Paul's next admonition reminds us that he is writing to a concrete community involved in a bitter dispute. His language compares the Galatians to wild beasts who begin by biting one another, then escalate to devouring and consuming one another (v. 15). They are using their freedom for self-indulgence rather than for the needs of the community. If they are to overcome "the desires of the flesh," then they must "live by the Spirit" (v. 16).

Living in the Spirit suggests a daily, progressive opening of one's life to the expansive love experienced in Christ. Paul contrasts this way of life to the way of the flesh. As Paul uses the term, "the flesh" does not mean the human body. It does not refer to physical desires, human feelings, or sensual pleasures, all of which are part of God's good creation. Rather, the flesh is those tendencies within human beings that are opposed to the Spirit, that is, our desire to turn in on ourselves and away from God. The Spirit and the flesh represent two different ways of living (v. 17). These two battle over a person's freedom, which is assured by the Spirit and thwarted by the flesh.

The "works of the flesh" (vv. 19–21) are all those actions that arise from a life opposed to the Spirit. Though they arise from within a person, they manifest themselves in a life that protects the self and dominates others. The "fruit of the Spirit" (vv. 22–23), in contrast, is the result of a life rooted in Christ. The Spirit's fruit is produced when the garden sown in human freedom receives the life-giving rain of the Holy Spirit.

This list of the Spirit's fruit can often be helpful in distinguishing genuine guidance of the Holy Spirit from our own subjective feelings and impulses. Though there is no foolproof method of discerning the Spirit's work, we can learn to recognize the fruit of the Spirit. If a choice or action is led by the Spirit, it will produce results such as love, joy, peace, generosity, and faithfulness. If a choice or action results in hostility, jealousy, anger, hatred, or dissension, there is a good chance the Spirit has nothing to do with it.

After listening for the Word of God in this text, try to answer this question:

✝ In what way is the whole law summed up in the commandment to love?

Meditatio

Spend some time meditating on the fruit of the Spirit and its growth in your life.

‡ Which fruit of the Spirit is beginning to bud in me? Which fruit is blossoming? Which is ripe for the harvest?

‡ How does our culture sometimes mistake genuine freedom for self-indulgence and gratifying the desires of the flesh? How can we preserve our God-given freedom?

‡ When have I tried to make an important decision by distinguishing the impulses of the Spirit from my own self-centered desires? How could the fruit of the Spirit help in that discernment?

Oratio

Pray to the Holy Spirit in whatever way seems to respond to the divine Word spoken to you through this text.

> Come, Holy Spirit. Produce in me the character traits of Jesus and kindle in me the fire of your love. Set me free to serve the needs of others. May your presence shine through me in love and joy, peace and patience, generosity and faithfulness.

Continue praying using the biblical vocabulary you have heard . . .

Contemplatio

When words are no longer necessary or helpful, just be silent in the presence of God. Ask the Holy Spirit to fill your heart with love.

Write a few words about your contemplative experience.

Operatio

What can I do to encourage the growth and maturation of the Spirit's fruit? How can I use my ripest fruit in the service of another today?

19

Proclaiming the Scandalous Message of the Cross

Lectio

In your quiet space, place a cross or crucifix near you as you read. Vocalize the words of the text so that you not only read with your eyes but also hear with your ears.

1 CORINTHIANS 1:17–31

[17]For Christ did not send me to baptize but to proclaim the gospel, and not with eloquent wisdom, so that the cross of Christ might not be emptied of its power.

[18]For the message about the cross is foolishness to those who are perishing, but to us who are being saved it is the power of God. [19]For it is written,

"I will destroy the wisdom of the wise,
and the discernment of the discerning I will thwart."

[20]Where is the one who is wise? Where is the scribe? Where is the debater of this age? Has not God made foolish the wisdom of the world? [21]For since, in the wisdom of God, the world did not know God through wisdom, God decided, through the foolishness of our proclamation, to save those who believe. [22]For Jews demand signs and Greeks desire wisdom, [23]but we proclaim Christ crucified, a stumbling

block to Jews and foolishness to Gentiles, [24]but to those who are the called, both Jews and Greeks, Christ the power of God and the wisdom of God. [25]For God's foolishness is wiser than human wisdom, and God's weakness is stronger than human strength.

[26]Consider your own call, brothers and sisters: not many of you were wise by human standards, not many were powerful, not many were of noble birth. [27]But God chose what is foolish in the world to shame the wise; God chose what is weak in the world to shame the strong; [28]God chose what is low and despised in the world, things that are not, to reduce to nothing things that are, [29]so that no one might boast in the presence of God. [30]He is the source of your life in Christ Jesus, who became for us wisdom from God, and righteousness and sanctification and redemption, [31]in order that, as it is written, "Let the one who boasts, boast in the Lord."

After hearing Paul's inspiring words, continue seeking the significance and meaning of this passage.

As Paul begins to present the content of his letter to the church in Corinth, he highlights the fact that his primary calling as an apostle is "to proclaim the gospel" (v. 17). The essence of the gospel, he explains, is God's saving work in the cross of Christ. It is a message that cannot be delivered with smooth and eloquent rhetoric because salvation through the rugged and torturous cross is an outrageous defiance of worldly expectations. The substance of the message determines the appropriate style of its presentation. The gospel is not a slickly packaged self-help scheme competing for attention with other popular ideas. It is the announcement of God's shocking intervention to save and transform the world.

"The message about the cross" divides humanity into two groups: those who are perishing, who reject this message as "foolishness," and those being saved, who receive it as "the power of God" (v. 18). Though the former divisions, Jew and Gentile, slave and free, woman and man, have dissolved in Christ, the judging and saving activity of God in the world is underway through the gospel. The church consists of those who are "being saved," a description that refers to a process that is not yet complete. Members of the church experience the power of God in the proclamation of the gospel and find themselves on a trajectory toward salvation.

In the logic of human wisdom, the cross seems embarrassing a
expresses the ultimate in human weakness, failure, humiliation
In a world where the cross was seen as the most horrid and barʋaᴉ.
of punishment imaginable, the gospel about a crucified Savior seemed to
be utter madness. Both Jews and Greeks considered the cross absurd.

Yet, in the crucifixion of his Son, God surpassed human wisdom and
acted powerfully to save us from sin and death. The meaning of the cross
was transformed by the person who was stretched out upon it and by the
God who "destroy[s] the wisdom of the wise" (v. 19). Now the cross expresses radical giving for others, hope in the midst of suffering, and ultimate
victory over the greatest evils, the powers of sin and death.

The Jews believed that if God were to visit the world with salvation, it
would be through great works of liberation. It was inconceivable that the
Messiah could suffer such a disgraceful and humiliating death.

The Gentile Greeks, on the other hand, sought to know God through
reasoned arguments. They followed those who used silver-tongued speech
and persuasive rhetoric. They could not conceive of a man having wisdom
yet not having sufficient wit to save himself from so ghastly a death.

It seemed that the Christian message had little chance of success among
the Jews or the Greeks. Yet, for those called by God, Jews and Greeks together, this mind-boggling paradox of the crucified Savior is "the power
of God and the wisdom of God" (v. 24). Here was truth that could not be
argued with reason or imposed with power. It had to be revealed by God,
which was the reason Paul received his call to proclaim the gospel of the
cross to an incredulous world longing for salvation.

Paul invites the Corinthians to reflect on their own unmerited calling as
a sign of how God overturns human expectations. Not many of them were
highly educated, powerful, or wealthy (v. 26). The fact that the early church
brought together people of diverse backgrounds and statuses, acknowledging one another as "brothers and sisters," was one of its most distinctive
features. This gathering of the foolish, weak, and lowly was modeled on
the pattern of Jesus's ministry. By creating a community made up of people
whom the world scorns, God has chosen to shame the wise, the strong,
and the powerful of the world (vv. 27–28). All boasting and self-assertion
must melt away before the presence of the wise and powerful God who is
our source of life in Jesus Christ.

Meditatio

Reflect on your own understanding of the cross. Repeat and ponder whatever words or phrases strike you from your reading.

‡ Because the cross has become such a common and conventional symbol in our culture, it has lost much of its effectiveness to stir our emotions. What would be the impact of the cross with its original power in our culture today?

‡ What is the impact of the cross on me when I reflect on its implication? How does the meaning of the cross defy logic and human understanding?

‡ Why would God choose to manifest himself in weakness, humiliation, and defeat? In what ways is the church a visible sign of how God turns the values of the world upside down?

Oratio

After reflecting on the cross and Paul's inspired words, respond in prayer using the language of Paul's letter.

Crucified Savior, help me to embrace the mystery of your cross at the center of my life. Though it seems foolish in the eyes of the world, I rejoice in the wisdom and power you proclaim in weakness. Make my life a sign of your radical and astonishing grace.

Continue praying to the one who has called you in weakness and humility to share in divine life . . .

Contemplatio

Sit in the presence of the cross and contemplate the wisdom and the power of God. Dispense with human logic, reason, and understanding. Just present yourself humbly in the presence of God.

Write a few words from your silent contemplation before the living God.

Operatio

Do I wear a cross on my body or display a cross in my home? How can I be more aware of the radical and countercultural sign I exhibit and the message I am proclaiming to others?

20

Paul's Style and
Motivation for Ministry

Lectio

Let this text welcome you into conversation with Paul. Imagine that he is speaking his heart to you and encouraging you to follow in his path.

1 CORINTHIANS 9:16–27

[16]If I proclaim the gospel, this gives me no ground for boasting, for an obligation is laid on me, and woe to me if I do not proclaim the gospel! [17]For if I do this of my own will, I have a reward; but if not of my own will, I am entrusted with a commission. [18]What then is my reward? Just this: that in my proclamation I may make the gospel free of charge, so as not to make full use of my rights in the gospel.

[19]For though I am free with respect to all, I have made myself a slave to all, so that I might win more of them. [20]To the Jews I became as a Jew, in order to win Jews. To those under the law I became as one under the law (though I myself am not under the law) so that I might win those under the law. [21]To those outside the law I became as one outside the law (though I am not free from God's law but am under Christ's law) so that I might win those outside the law. [22]To the weak I became weak, so that I might win the weak. I have become all

How can we be a slave to all?

things to all people, that I might by all means save some. ²³I do it all for the sake of the gospel, so that I may share in its blessings.

²⁴Do you not know that in a race the runners all compete, but only one receives the prize? Run in such a way that you may win it. ²⁵Athletes exercise self-control in all things; they do it to receive a perishable wreath, but we an imperishable one. ²⁶So I do not run aimlessly, nor do I box as though beating the air; ²⁷but I punish my body and enslave it, so that after proclaiming to others I myself should not be disqualified.

After considering these words of Paul and letting them touch your heart, continue to explore the text through these comments:

Paul offers his readers a look at his own interior motivation for ministry. He proclaims the gospel not by his own choice but because God has sent him forth to do so. On the Damascus road he was "entrusted with a commission." He is unable to boast in his ministry as an apostle any more than a slave could boast of his obedience to his master's commands (vv. 16–17).

Paul states that even though he has the right to earn a living through his preaching, receiving a material reward for his ministry, he has chosen to forego his rights and offer the gospel "free of charge" (v. 18). In this way, his service follows the pattern of the gospel itself. Christ himself became a slave for all by his sacrificial life and death. Paul's "reward," then, is being able to offer his life to God and to others in the pattern of Christ.

In describing the method of his mission, Paul states that his all-consuming concern is to "win" as many people as possible for the gospel (v. 19). To achieve this goal, he adapts his behavior in whatever way is necessary to overcome ethnic and cultural divisions. Paul's desire is to bring all people— Jew and Gentile, slave and free, woman and man—into the one community of faith in Christ. To achieve that end, even though he is a free man, he has made himself "a slave to all."

Paul offers examples of the ways he submits himself to the cultural structures and practices of the people he hopes to reach with the gospel (vv. 20–22). When in the company of Jews, he takes on their law-observant patterns of living. Though he knows he is no longer bound to the works of the Jewish law, he reverts to his law-observant way of living for their sake.

When he was among the Gentiles, he conforms his life to the Greek ways, clarifying that he always follows the law of Christ. Likewise, "to the weak," he says, "I became weak." With those weak in faith or scrupulous in their religious practices, he makes sure to avoid any scandal, any practice that would make it more difficult to lead them toward an appreciation of Christian freedom. With those weak in social status, he takes on their lifestyle, becoming a manual laborer and refusing the patronage of the wealthy.

In summary, Paul states, "I have become all things to all people, that I might by all means save some" (v. 22). Paul's adaptability appeared to some of his critics as inconsistency or even hypocrisy. However, Paul makes it clear to his readers that his versatility in ministry was aimed at a consistent goal: "I do it all for the sake of the gospel" (v. 23). He does whatever he can to most effectively fulfill his commission as Christ's apostle. The gospel is not relativized to social conditions; rather, Paul himself is relativized in order to preserve the integrity of the gospel he proclaims.

After describing his own motivation for ministry, Paul concludes with a grand exhortation to his readers, comparing the Christian life to that of runners and boxers (vv. 24–27). Paul frequently uses athletic metaphors in his letters, and this one is particularly relevant for his readers because Corinth was the site of the famous Isthmian Games. As runners compete to complete the race and win the prize, Christians should live a disciplined life, focused on the things that ultimately matter. As boxers punish and enslave their own bodies in order to make every punch count, Christians should subject themselves to disciplined self-control and devote themselves to service. If the athletes in the Greek games competed to win a garland of withering leaves, how much more should Christians strive to win an imperishable crown!

After exploring the motivations for Paul's preaching the gospel, consider this question:

‡ What does Paul mean when he says, "I have become all things to all people" (v. 22)?

Meditatio

Consider what Paul is teaching you about the Christian life as he discusses the motives and methods of his ministry.

‡ What characteristic of Paul's style and method of ministry do I most admire? What aspects could I adopt for my own life in Christ?

‡ Paul said, "I have become all things to all people." In what way is this quote a description of my own life? How does my motive compare to Paul's? How could I grow in my ability to contextualize myself for the sake of my discipleship?

‡ Paul compared his ministry to running and boxing. What athletic event is most like my Christian life? What are the comparisons?

Oratio

Speak to God in response to the words, ideas, and images of your reading.
Offer to God what you have discovered about yourself from your meditation.

Lord God, you commissioned Paul to preach the gospel and instilled in him a zeal for mission. Help me to imitate his passion for Christ, his dedication to serving others, and his focused attention to the things that matter in life. Help me to run the race and seek the imperishable crown of your presence.

Continue pouring out your prayer to God until words are no longer necessary or useful . . .

Contemplatio

Athletes usually spend some quiet time before competition contemplating their goal. Take some time to consider your life's purpose and focus on the things that matter most.

Write a few words about your experience of focused contemplatio.

Operatio

What would it mean to me to apply Paul's method from verses 19–23 to bring the gospel to others around me? In what one situation could I adapt my lifestyle and patterns of living to help another encounter Christ?

21

The Unity and Diversity
of the Spirit's Gifts

Listen to Paul as he speaks to the early church and to the church today about the contribution of each person to the body of Christ in the world.

1 CORINTHIANS 12:1–13

[1]Now concerning spiritual gifts, brothers and sisters, I do not want you to be uninformed. [2]You know that when you were pagans, you were enticed and led astray to idols that could not speak. [3]Therefore I want you to understand that no one speaking by the Spirit of God ever says "Let Jesus be cursed!" and no one can say "Jesus is Lord" except by the Holy Spirit.

[4]Now there are varieties of gifts, but the same Spirit; [5]and there are varieties of services, but the same Lord; [6]and there are varieties of activities, but it is the same God who activates all of them in everyone. [7]To each is given the manifestation of the Spirit for the common good. [8]To one is given through the Spirit the utterance of wisdom, and to another the utterance of knowledge according to the same Spirit, [9]to another faith by the same Spirit, to another gifts of healing by the one Spirit, [10]to another the working of miracles, to another prophecy, to another the discernment of spirits, to another various kinds of tongues, to another the interpretation of tongues.

¹¹All these are activated by one and the same Spirit, who allots to each one individually just as the Spirit chooses.

¹²For just as the body is one and has many members, and all the members of the body, though many, are one body, so it is with Christ. ¹³For in the one Spirit we were all baptized into one body—Jews or Greeks, slaves or free—and we were all made to drink of one Spirit.

Let Paul's inspired words enter your mind and heart, then continue to explore his message and meaning through these remarks:

Paul describes the gifts that fill the church as "charisms," manifestations of God's grace. These gifts are freely given to individual believers, and they are activated in each person by the Holy Spirit. Paul describes a church filled with charisms, in which all the members contribute their own unique gifts for building up the whole community. The power of God's Spirit is palpably present, working through the many complementary gifts of each member of the community.

Paul wanted the community in Corinth to understand that merely expressing a sign of the spiritual world, like the ecstatic utterances of those who worship pagan idols, does not indicate a true gift from God's Spirit (vv. 1–2). The Corinthians were getting caught up in the thrill of the emotional experience rather than seeking to honor God. The first criterion of a genuine gift from the Holy Spirit is that the person confesses "Jesus is Lord" (v. 3). This acknowledgment of Jesus's lordship, lived authentically in a person's life, indicates that a person is living in the realm of the Spirit's power. The second criterion of an authentic gift is that it is exercised "for the common good" of the community (v. 7). Gifts of the Spirit are not given for the personal glorification or status of the one receiving them. A genuine gift must be oriented toward the growth and well-being of those called to be the church, forming a unifying purpose for the differing gifts.

This unified purpose of the variety of gifts is rooted in the divine origins of each believer's gift. In three parallel statements, Paul states that there are "varieties of gifts, but the same Spirit"; "varieties of services, but the same Lord"; and "varieties of activities, but . . . the same God who activates all of them in everyone" (vv. 4–6). The rich diversity of the divine presence among believers—experienced as Spirit, Lord, and God—is the foundation for the abundant variety of gifts in the church. The many gifts, services, and activities manifest God's own multifaceted-yet-unified presence among believers.

Paul gives examples of these manifestations of the Spirit, though his list is not exhaustive, since other lists of gifts are found in other letters of Paul (vv. 8–10). The same community that prized the intellectual gift of uttering wisdom also valued the highly emotional gift of speaking in tongues. Healings, miracles, and prophetic speech seemed to be regular events within the community. This rich diversity of spiritual gifts within the individual members of the church was "activated by one and the same Spirit" (v. 11).

Paul summarizes his teaching about the church's unity within great diversity by using the metaphor of the body. He uses this image to describe the multiplicity, interdependence, and importance of all members of the church. Yet, Paul compares the community not only to the body but essentially to Christ himself: "so it is with Christ" (v. 12). The great variety of believers is bound in a living unity with the risen Christ. In him, the great diversity of the community and its many gifts become purposeful and beneficial. This unity in the body of Christ is realized through the work of the Holy Spirit: "In the one Spirit we were all baptized into one body" (v. 13). Through the power of the Spirit, even extreme ethnic and social incompatibility—Jews or Greeks, slaves or free people—is superseded and overcome when believers are baptized into Christ.

After hearing Paul's description of the early church, try to answer these questions:

‡ What was the problem or abuse in Corinth that necessitated Paul's teaching about spiritual gifts?

‡ What are the criteria for discerning genuine gifts of the Spirit? Why does Paul stress the importance of these criteria?

Meditatio

Reflect on the words of these texts as if they were spoken to you. Allow the words to affirm your role in the church and the importance of your unique contribution.

✠ What is the source of the church's unity? Why does Paul encourage unity rather than uniformity within the church? What is the difference?

✠ How does Paul's teaching challenge my understanding of the workings of the Holy Spirit within Christ's church? What point do I want to remember most?

✠ In what way does Paul's teaching affirm my own unique contribution to the church? What gifts, services, or activities have I been called to offer?

Oratio

Respond to God's Word to you with your own words to God. Speak from your heart in response to the hope you have been offered.

Spirit, Lord, and God, you distribute and empower gifts, services, and activities throughout the church. Break down the divisions that separate people from one another and unite them with a deep desire to serve one another in love.

Continue to express your hopes, desires, struggles, and commitment . . .

Contemplatio

Though you sit alone, realize that you are a part of the worldwide body of Christ. Try to feel the church members' joys and struggles as connected to your own.

Write a few words about the feelings that fill your heart.

Operatio

How effective am I at recognizing the gifts of others? What could I do today to affirm the gifts I see in another person?

22

Holding Firmly to What Is of First Importance

Read carefully this passage that Paul says is "of first importance." Consider how you can "hold firmly to the message," as Paul instructs.

1 CORINTHIANS 15:1–19

¹Now I would remind you, brothers and sisters, of the good news that I proclaimed to you, which you in turn received, in which also you stand, ²through which also you are being saved, if you hold firmly to the message that I proclaimed to you—unless you have come to believe in vain.

³For I handed on to you as of first importance what I in turn had received: that Christ died for our sins in accordance with the scriptures, ⁴and that he was buried, and that he was raised on the third day in accordance with the scriptures, ⁵and that he appeared to Cephas, then to the twelve. ⁶Then he appeared to more than five hundred brothers and sisters at one time, most of whom are still alive, though some have died. ⁷Then he appeared to James, then to all the apostles. ⁸Last of all, as to one untimely born, he appeared also to me. ⁹For I am the least of the apostles, unfit to be called an apostle,

because I persecuted the church of God. [10]But by the grace of God I am what I am, and his grace toward me has not been in vain. On the contrary, I worked harder than any of them—though it was not I, but the grace of God that is with me. [11]Whether then it was I or they, so we proclaim and so you have come to believe.

[12]Now if Christ is proclaimed as raised from the dead, how can some of you say there is no resurrection of the dead? [13]If there is no resurrection of the dead, then Christ has not been raised; [14]and if Christ has not been raised, then our proclamation has been in vain and your faith has been in vain. [15]We are even found to be misrepresenting God, because we testified of God that he raised Christ—whom he did not raise if it is true that the dead are not raised. [16]For if the dead are not raised, then Christ has not been raised. [17]If Christ has not been raised, your faith is futile and you are still in your sins. [18]Then those also who have died in Christ have perished. [19]If for this life only we have hoped in Christ, we are of all people most to be pitied.

After listening for the message of Paul's exhortation, carefully consider the significance of his words by reading these comments:

At the heart of Paul's ministry, both his preaching and his letters, is the resurrection of Jesus Christ. Before his conversion, Paul, like most Jews of his day, shared a distant hope of bodily resurrection in the final age. But after encountering the risen Lord, Paul knew that this glorious new existence, foretold by the prophets and sages of Israel, had suddenly and unexpectedly begun in Jesus. This section of Paul's letter is the most extended discussion of resurrection in the Bible.

The Good News of the Christian faith can be summarized in a few brief phrases. Paul expresses it in a formula that he "received" from the apostles and "handed on" to the church: Christ died for our sins and was buried; Christ was raised from the dead and appeared to his disciples (vv. 3–5). He says that this early statement of Christian belief is "of first importance" (v. 3), Christian faith in a nutshell.

Paul insists that Christ died and was raised "in accordance with the scriptures" (vv. 3–4). Because no Old Testament texts specifically anticipate the death or resurrection of the Messiah, the foundation of Paul's claim is most likely the witness of the Old Testament as a whole. God's care for creation, fidelity to the covenant, unwavering love for his people, and power over all opposing forces are scriptural themes that lead up to their culmination in Christ's death and resurrection. God's rescue of humanity from sin and death through Christ is the final phase of the story of salvation for ancient Israel.

Paul's listing of specific people to whom the risen Lord appeared, first to Peter and the twelve, followed by five hundred men and women, then James and all the apostles (vv. 5–7), indicates that the resurrection was real, just as the burial of Jesus indicates that his death was real. The appearance of the risen Christ was not just a deep, subjective experience or an inexpressible encounter apart from this world. There was still in Paul's day a convincing number of witnesses willing to testify that they had seen Jesus alive.

Paul adds his own witness to Christ's resurrection to the list of others, yet Paul notes that his was "last of all" (v. 8). When Paul saw the risen Christ, the appearances were at an end. By claiming that his own witness was the last, Paul distinguishes the appearances of the risen Christ in the apostolic age from every latter type of subjective vision and personal experience of Jesus. He compares his own experience to "[some]one untimely born" (v. 8). He was not ready for his own new birth.

Paul's teaching on resurrection was prompted by some of the Corinthians who were saying "there is no resurrection of the dead" (v. 12). The Greek view that dominated most of the world at the time was a dualistic understanding of the human person—an immortal soul imprisoned within a body that dies and corrupts. Contrary to this position, Paul insists that the whole human person, created by God, will be given a new, transformed bodily life through the resurrection of the dead when Christ returns. Paul develops his argument and its consequence point by point, for without the resurrection, Christianity is only a system of delusions and futile human fantasy, leaving its adherents "most to be pitied" (v. 19).

After carefully reading Paul's text and the commentary, answer this question about your reading:

‡ What does Paul do to convince his readers that the resurrection of Jesus is real?

Meditatio

Hold firmly to Paul's message by carefully reflecting on his message in terms of your own life in Christ.

✝ In what sense does Paul testify that the death and resurrection of Jesus was "in accordance with the scriptures" (v. 3)? How does the Old Testament demonstrate that the death and resurrection of Jesus was the final phase of God's saving plan?

✝ Paul urges us to "hold firmly" (v. 2) to his synthesis of the gospel. How do concise statements of belief help prevent me from losing my grip on the gospel message?

✝ Why is resurrection the core of Christian belief? What would our faith be like if Jesus had not been raised from the dead?

Oratio

Give praise and thanks to God for the gift and wonder of Christ's resurrection. Speak words that express whatever new hope or purpose you have discovered.

> Lord God, you transformed the heart of Paul through his experience of your risen Son. I too live in you as a result of your grace. Give me a fresh experience of your merciful love today and help me to witness to the goodness you have poured into my life through Christ's resurrection.

Continue to express your prayer to God with a heart full of faith . . .

Contemplatio

Be still, realizing that without Christ you are trapped in sin and destined for eternal death. Be grateful that you can live in joyful and confident hope.

Write a few words describing the gratitude you feel.

Operatio

Because of Christ's resurrection my life has meaning and purpose. I know that in the Lord my labor is not in vain. What can I do today to live and celebrate the new hope that Christ has given me through his resurrection?

23

A Precious Treasure in Fragile Vessels

As you study this text and commentary, highlight or underline the parts you wish to remember and return to for reflection. Let the Holy Spirit guide your careful reading.

2 CORINTHIANS 4:1–11

[1]Therefore, since it is by God's mercy that we are engaged in this ministry, we do not lose heart. [2]We have renounced the shameful things that one hides; we refuse to practice cunning or to falsify God's Word; but by the open statement of the truth we commend ourselves to the conscience of everyone in the sight of God. [3]And even if our gospel is veiled, it is veiled to those who are perishing. [4]In their case the god of this world has blinded the minds of the unbelievers, to keep them from seeing the light of the gospel of the glory of Christ, who is the image of God. [5]For we do not proclaim ourselves; we proclaim Jesus Christ as Lord and ourselves as your slaves for Jesus' sake. [6]For it is the God who said, "Let light shine out of darkness," who has shone in our hearts to give the light of the knowledge of the glory of God in the face of Jesus Christ.

⁷But we have this treasure in clay jars, so that it may be made clear that this extraordinary power belongs to God and does not come from us. ⁸We are afflicted in every way, but not crushed; perplexed, but not driven to despair; ⁹persecuted, but not forsaken; struck down, but not destroyed; ¹⁰always carrying in the body the death of Jesus, so that the life of Jesus may also be made visible in our bodies. ¹¹For while we live, we are always being given up to death for Jesus' sake, so that the life of Jesus may be made visible in our mortal flesh.

Let Paul's words sink into your mind and heart, then continue to listen to the text through the church's teaching and scholarship.

Paul offers his readers a profound and intimate understanding of his own ministry and his reasons for carrying on in the midst of all the distressing experiences he has to undergo in discharging it. First and foremost, Paul knows that his ministry is not something he merited or earned. It originated as a gift of God's mercy (v. 1). Having been called and commissioned by God, he is a confident minister of the gospel. He rejects any cunning or deceptive practices, behaviors that he considers unworthy of the gospel (v. 2). Rather, he ministers in openness and honesty, refusing to compromise the truth of God's Word. Since it was God's action that changed his heart and drew him to be an apostle, he could not be other than faithful to God's mission and ready to carry on without losing heart. As a herald for the gospel, Paul does not draw attention to himself but to its essence—"Jesus Christ as Lord" (v. 5). Since Jesus is Lord of Paul's life and of the church, Paul likens his own work to that of "slaves for Jesus's sake."

It seems that there were those in the community of Corinth who maintained that Paul's message lacked the clarity and eloquence of a true revelation from God. Paul admits that the gospel he preaches appears "veiled" to some, but he asserts that it is hidden only to those who refuse to see the saving truth that God offers (v. 3). These have been blinded by the evil powers of this world, which keep them from "seeing the light of the gospel" (v. 4). The ability to "see" the truth of God's Word is always the result of both God's gracious working within us as well as our removal of whatever blinders we have placed in the way.

Paul uses the biblical image of "light" to speak about the glorious gospel of Christ: "the light of the gospel of the glory of Christ, who is the image of God" (v. 4) and "the light of the knowledge of the glory of God in the face of Jesus Christ" (v. 6). Paul is overwhelmed with the wondrous and brilliant revelation to which he is entrusted—hardly a veiled message. On the road to Damascus, that light, the glory of Christ, first shone in his heart. The same God who said at creation, "Let light shine out of darkness," has given to Paul and the whole world the light of the new creation. This creator God has shone his light into the hearts of believers. The gospel is light and brings insight and understanding to those who remove the veil and open their hearts to it.

Everything about Paul's mission demonstrates that he is not the light but that he is a fragile vessel, a "clay jar," that contains "this treasure" (v. 7). Paul's weakness and frailty attest to the fact that the gospel of Christ is empowered by God and not himself. This power within him is demonstrated by four vivid contrasts (vv. 8–9). He ought to be crushed, driven to despair, forsaken, and destroyed because of his suffering for the gospel. But Paul's trials attest to his union with Christ, whose suffering and death are being replicated in his own life. He is carrying in his own body "the death of Jesus" (v. 10); he is "being given up to death for Jesus' sake" (v. 11). But Paul's dying with Jesus in frailty and suffering also manifests "the life of Jesus" (v. 11) made visible in his mortal body. He experiences an indestructible power that is not his own, that always bears him up and suffuses his present existence with visible signs of the resurrection for which he waits in hope.

After studying this text and commentary, respond to these questions to review your understanding:

‡ Why does Paul use the image of the fragile vessel to describe himself?

‡ What does Paul mean by "carrying in the body the death of Jesus" (v. 10)?

Meditatio

*Reread and reflect on the verses and sentences you highlighted during your
lectio. Bring your insights to respond to the following questions:*

‡ Paul knows that God will never forsake those he has called to ministry
because that work is given through the gift of God's mercy. How does
this understanding of my own responsibilities help sustain me in difficult times?

‡ Paul refers to the gospel of Christ as a "light" (v. 4) and a "treasure" (v. 7).
In what ways do these images help me better understand and appreciate
my calling as a minister of Christ in the world?

‡ When have I felt Christ working within me even though I was convinced
I was not equal to the task before me? How am I able to make the life of
Christ visible within my own mortal life?

Oratio

Respond in prayer to Paul's explanation of the Christian life. Offer up your sufferings in union with the dying of Jesus.

Faithful God, you called Paul to be a minister of the gospel and to proclaim the truth of your Word. Help me to experience the treasure of the gospel in the fragile vessel of my life so that others may see its light and live.

Continue this prayer in words that issue from your heart . . .

Contemplatio

Picture your life as a fragile clay jar containing the light of Christ. Sit with that image for a while and realize that God is transforming you from within through the gift of faith.

Write a few words about your contemplative experience.

Operatio

There is no escape from the process of dying. But if we join our dying to that of Christ, the life of Christ will also be manifest within us and in the lives of those we serve. How can I begin to live more consciously with this truth in mind?

24

Boasting in Weakness,
Living with Strength

Lectio

Read Paul's agitated words to the Corinthians aloud. You might want to try pacing back and forth as you read, imagining Paul's passionate convictions.

2 CORINTHIANS 11:21–30; 12:7–10

²¹But whatever anyone dares to boast of—I am speaking as a fool—I also dare to boast of that. ²²Are they Hebrews? So am I. Are they Israelites? So am I. Are they descendants of Abraham? So am I. ²³Are they ministers of Christ? I am talking like a madman—I am a better one: with far greater labors, far more imprisonments, with countless floggings, and often near death. ²⁴Five times I have received from the Jews the forty lashes minus one. ²⁵Three times I was beaten with rods. Once I received a stoning. Three times I was shipwrecked; for a night and a day I was adrift at sea; ²⁶on frequent journeys, in danger from rivers, danger from bandits, danger from my own people, danger from Gentiles, danger in the city, danger in the wilderness, danger at sea, danger from false brothers and sisters; ²⁷in toil and hardship, through many a sleepless night, hungry and thirsty, often without food, cold and naked. ²⁸And, besides other

things, I am under daily pressure because of my anxiety for all the churches. ²⁹Who is weak, and I am not weak? Who is made to stumble, and I am not indignant?

³⁰If I must boast, I will boast of the things that show my weakness.

⁷Therefore, to keep me from being too elated, a thorn was given me in the flesh, a messenger of Satan to torment me, to keep me from being too elated. ⁸Three times I appealed to the Lord about this, that it would leave me, ⁹but he said to me, "My grace is sufficient for you, for power is made perfect in weakness." So, I will boast all the more gladly of my weaknesses, so that the power of Christ may dwell in me. ¹⁰Therefore I am content with weaknesses, insults, hardships, persecutions, and calamities for the sake of Christ; for whenever I am weak, then I am strong.

After listening for God's Word through Paul, continue listening for the insights and message of the Scripture.

Paul's opponents in Corinth were apparently boasting of their powerful feats and notable accomplishments in order to win over the people to their side. They must have challenged Paul to present his own credentials as an apostle. Paul refuses to take the competition seriously and parodies his opponents in their foolish boasts (11:21).

The contest of fools begins with a focus on titles. Here Paul can equally claim the titles of his Jewish heritage: Hebrew, Israelite, and descendant of Abraham (11:22). But when it comes to the next title, "minister of Christ," he states, "I am a better one" (11:23). Paul cleverly pulls the rug out from under his opponents. Feigning a madman, he stakes his claim to the title based not on honors won but on torments endured. These boasts are doubly foolish, since boasting itself is foolish, and, by his opponents' standards, suffering and weakness do not count as commendable qualities.

Lists of accomplishments were common in Paul's world, and the Roman emperors set up inscriptions in public places listing their achievements. Paul can write as long and impressive a list as any of them. The weaknesses and trials that Paul's opponents used to discredit his authority, Paul now brazenly showcases. Paul's extraordinary list includes sufferings he bore at the hands of others as well as the perils endured by travelers in those days (11:23–27), showing the extent that Paul suffered for the sake of the gospel.

In addition to his physical sufferings, Paul notes the inward pain of stress on his mind and heart (11: 28). Many sleepless nights arose from his anxiety about one or another of the many churches he had founded. Throughout the Mediterranean world, each church had its own particular problems and concerns, which were continually reported to him. Like a loving parent, Paul felt responsible for each community, but he was often unable to do anything because travel was slow and distances were great.

Paul's final witness to his weakness is what he calls the thorn in the flesh (12:7). It is impossible to know what particular suffering Paul is referring to here. It is clearly a painful affliction, either physical, mental, or spiritual. He also calls his malady "a messenger of Satan" sent to bring him torment. Paul has in mind the affliction of Job, whose faithfulness was tested with pain and torment through the instrument of "Satan" (Job 1:6–12). Though we don't know the exact nature of the hardship, we do know its purpose. Paul twice emphasizes that it was given to prevent him "from being too elated" (12:7). Like Job, his affliction saved him from spiritual pride and was an instrument of his greater understanding of God. Helping Paul realize the limits of his human condition and the wonders of God's grace, the thorn served to advance the gospel.

Before Paul understood the thorn's purpose, he prayed "three times" for it to leave him (12:8). Like Jesus at Gethsemane, who pleaded with God three times to take away his cup of suffering and then came to accept God's purposes, Paul came to understand his affliction as serving God's saving plan. As in the suffering of his Son, God used Paul's suffering for a greater good. Paul states the lesson he learned as a revelation from God: "My grace is sufficient for you, for power is made perfect in weakness" (12:9). It was not only a lesson received by Paul but also a revealed truth that could be applied to the experience of all Christians. When we accept the limitations of our existence, we permit the grace of God to operate more fully within us and to be seen by others more clearly.

A remarkable portrait of Paul emerges from this catalog of hardships endured for Christ. Countless untold stories of courage and compassion lie behind this list. Yet, Paul's severe suffering left no hint of resentment or bitterness. It was Christ who lived within him, giving him fervor, joy, and hope.

Meditatio

After thinking about how Paul's words addressed his first readers, reflect on their impact in your own life. As you bring God's Word into the present context of your life, spend some time meditating on these questions:

‡ Why does Paul state he is speaking as a fool during his boasting. What seems to be his emotional state during this foolish boasting? How can humor sometimes help us through life's sufferings?

‡ How can suffering be a truer witness to Christian authority than fine speech and impressive accomplishments? In what ways can I claim suffering as a witness to my life in Christ?

‡ In the lives of both Jesus and Paul, their sufferings were seen by some as weaknesses. What insights does Paul offer to help me with my life's challenges?

Oratio

Having listened to Paul's account of his sufferings and his understanding of its fruit, respond now to God in the context of your own life with the words of Paul and the words of your heart.

> Giver of all grace, you called Paul to live for Christ and to suffer for the gospel. In the context of my own struggles, help me to understand that your grace is all I need and that your power is made perfect through my weakness. Grant me the insight of your Spirit to believe in your saving plan and to see all my life in the light of your will.

Continue speaking to God through the grace of Christ . . .

Contemplatio

Choose a short phrase from the Scripture, such as "My grace is sufficient for you," as your mantra during contemplatio. Slowly speak or chant the mantra as you experience the power of Christ dwelling within you.

Write a few words that arise from your contemplative experience of Christ's power within you.

Operatio

The more we can acknowledge and understand our own weakness, the more the power of Christ can work within it. What are some specific ways I can live out this truth so as to be a clearer instrument of God's grace for others?

25

Paul Addresses God's Beloved in Rome

Kiss the words of the biblical text and ask God to let the inspired words speak powerfully to your spirit today. Read the words aloud and listen to Paul speak to you.

ROMANS 1:1–15

[1]Paul, a servant of Jesus Christ, called to be an apostle, set apart for the gospel of God, [2]which he promised beforehand through his prophets in the holy scriptures, [3]the gospel concerning his Son, who was descended from David according to the flesh [4]and was declared to be Son of God with power according to the spirit of holiness by resurrection from the dead, Jesus Christ our Lord, [5]through whom we have received grace and apostleship to bring about the obedience of faith among all the Gentiles for the sake of his name, [6]including yourselves who are called to belong to Jesus Christ,

[7]To all God's beloved in Rome, who are called to be saints:

Grace to you and peace from God our Father and the Lord Jesus Christ.

[8]First, I thank my God through Jesus Christ for all of you, because your faith is proclaimed throughout the world. [9]For God, whom I serve

with my spirit by announcing the gospel of his Son, is my witness that without ceasing I remember you always in my prayers, [10]asking that by God's will I may somehow at last succeed in coming to you. [11]For I am longing to see you so that I may share with you some spiritual gift to strengthen you— [12]or rather so that we may be mutually encouraged by each other's faith, both yours and mine. [13]I want you to know, brothers and sisters, that I have often intended to come to you (but thus far have been prevented), in order that I may reap some harvest among you as I have among the rest of the Gentiles. [14]I am a debtor both to Greeks and to barbarians, both to the wise and to the foolish [15]—hence my eagerness to proclaim the gospel to you also who are in Rome.

Let Paul's words penetrate your mind and heart, then continue to explore the meaning and message of his letter.

As Paul pens this monumental letter to "God's beloved in Rome," he is writing to a church that he neither founded nor visited. Unlike his other letters, in which he writes to communities who know him well and addresses pastoral concerns of those churches, he writes here to the Christians in a city he has never seen. He writes to the church in Rome primarily to prepare them for his intended visit. Paul has carried out his task of preaching in the eastern Mediterranean world, and now he is ready to undertake the proclamation of the gospel in the western half of that world. He hopes to make Rome, the imperial capital of the Roman world, the base of his future mission. This letter is both his personal introduction to the church in Rome and an exposition of the theology he has developed.

Paul introduces himself and expands the usual salutation in order to establish credibility with the Romans, describing his apostleship and giving a brief summary of the faith. As a "servant of Jesus Christ," Paul is aligned with other servants of the Lord—Moses, Joshua, David, and the prophets—and inserted into the biblical history of salvation. As "apostle," Paul is aligned with the Twelve, personally called and sent by Christ, "set apart" by God at his conversion to proclaim the gospel.

This gospel for which Paul is sent had been "promised beforehand" by God "through his prophets in the holy scriptures" (v. 2). Throughout human history, the constant energy of God's love had been lighting up the darkness, desiring to bring salvation to the lost. The Good News of Jesus Christ is the goal of Israel's long history as described in the Scriptures. Apart from him, all that God had done was incomplete. The prophets had communicated God's promise of a final liberation, and now God has spoken his last word, the gospel of Christ.

Paul includes within his salutation a brief creed, a summary of the faith (vv. 3–4). The content of the gospel is essentially Jesus Christ, who was revealed as Son of God in two stages. According to his human nature, he was born from the royal house of David, the Messiah promised by God to Israel. According to the Holy Spirit, he was declared as Son of God with power through his resurrection from the dead. As descendant of David, Jesus was Son of God in humility and suffering; as Son of God in power, he entered his role as the exalted Lord. In his earthly ministry, he was God's suffering servant; in his heavenly reign, he is the glorious Lord Jesus Christ.

After describing the gospel's content, Paul describes his own distinctive call and gift of grace (v. 5). He is the apostle charged with the unique responsibility of bringing about the "obedience of faith" among the Gentiles. As Peter was "entrusted with the gospel for the circumcised," Paul was "entrusted with the gospel for the uncircumcised" (Gal. 2:7–8). Through these two pillars of the faith, all the nations can come into the community of salvation, including the people of Rome, and become the one people of God (vv. 6–7).

Paul then expresses his thankfulness to God for the Roman Christians and conveys his gratitude that the gospel has been received in the capital of the ancient world (v. 8). He testifies that the quality of their faith is an inspiration for the communities scattered across the Greco-Roman world. Though Paul can take no credit for their fame, they have been close to his heart, and he has felt a long-standing sense of responsibility to them. For many years he has drawn them and his desire to visit them into his constant prayer.

After listening to the introduction of Paul's letter with the ear of your heart, answer this question about the Scripture passage you have read:

✝ Why does Paul expand the introduction of his letter to the Romans with statements of his credentials and theology?

Meditatio

Imagine yourself in the imperial capital of Rome, receiving this letter from Paul. Then ask yourself what significance this has for you two thousand years later.

‡ What seem to be some of the major reasons Paul desired to visit Rome? What are some of the ways Christians could begin to evangelize our culture today?

‡ The "obedience of faith," the phrase that both begins (1:5) and ends (16:26) Paul's letter, expresses the requirement for entering the community of salvation. It shows that in Paul's understanding there is no separation between faith and obedience, believing and doing. How does this deepen my understanding of salvation through faith?

‡ The origin of Paul's apostleship was grace, the incomprehensible fact that God loves us despite our rebelliousness. In what ways has grace been the source of my Christian calling?

Oratio

Paul tells the Christians in Rome that he remembers them always in his prayers. Who and what do you want to remember in prayer today?

> Lord God, I pray for the people of my city, my church, and my family. You have led us to yourself through the power at work in the gospel and have called us to belong to Jesus Christ. Continue to strengthen us in faith and help us to be mutually encouraged by the faith of one another.

Continue to pray in whatever words arise from your own heart . . .

Contemplatio

Choose a word or phrase from Paul's letter to help you continue to focus on God's presence with you through his Word. Draw upon that word during your time of quiet contemplation.

Describe your contemplative time in a few summary words.

Operatio

Paul's letter gave strength and understanding to the people of Rome. In what way do I expect to be formed and changed in the coming days through studying this letter?

26

Jews and Gentiles
Justified by Faith

As you read Paul's teaching, highlight or underline passages that seem most pertinent to you. Ask God's Spirit to lead you to a practical understanding of these truths.

ROMANS 3:21–31

²¹But now, apart from law, the righteousness of God has been disclosed, and is attested by the law and the prophets, ²²the righteousness of God through faith in Jesus Christ for all who believe. For there is no distinction, ²³since all have sinned and fall short of the glory of God; ²⁴they are now justified by his grace as a gift, through the redemption that is in Christ Jesus, ²⁵whom God put forward as a sacrifice of atonement by his blood, effective through faith. He did this to show his righteousness, because in his divine forbearance he had passed over the sins previously committed; ²⁶it was to prove at the present time that he himself is righteous and that he justifies the one who has faith in Jesus.

²⁷Then what becomes of boasting? It is excluded. By what law? By that of works? No, but by the law of faith. ²⁸For we hold that a person is justified by faith apart from works prescribed by the law.

²⁹Or is God the God of Jews only? Is he not the God of Gentiles also? Yes, of Gentiles also, ³⁰since God is one; and he will justify the circumcised on the ground of faith and the uncircumcised through that same faith. ³¹Do we then overthrow the law by this faith? By no means! On the contrary, we uphold the law.

Having read Paul's words, continue to mark this commentary as you seek Paul's message.

The letter to the Romans contains Paul's most developed understanding of how God's salvation is offered to the world. "Righteousness" is a term rooted in the Old Testament that is used first as a characteristic of God. God's righteousness is shown as he offers rebellious Israel a judgment that is right and just. When Paul proclaims that now "the righteousness of God has been disclosed" (v. 21), he declares that a new era of God's plan has begun with the coming of Jesus, whose mission was to make known the righteousness of God in a new way. Jesus Christ is the personal manifestation of God's righteousness. Through God's faithful love made known in Jesus, God took the initiative to restore humanity to a right relationship with himself and to offer hope for salvation. Though humanity stands justly condemned, God's final verdict is not condemnation but acquittal.

This new era of salvation in Jesus Christ is "apart from law," that is, unattainable by human efforts, neither by following the laws of the Torah for the Jews nor by following a law of nature for the Greeks. It comes solely from God's initiative and is totally unearned and undeserved. Any human effort based on a code of law is woefully insufficient to attain what God offers to humanity in Christ.

Righteousness, or justification, must then be received and taken possession of by human beings through a relationship of "faith in Jesus Christ" (v. 22). Faith implies an acceptance of what we have received and the acknowledgment of Christ's lordship in our life. It leads to a dedication and a commitment to Christ that progressively intensify. This same response of faith is required of all people, Jew and Greek alike. "There is no distinction," Paul says, since all people have sinned and are in need of God's grace (v. 23). The cross is God's universal answer to humanity's universal need. The whole process of salvation is a gift of God, motivated by God's grace (v. 24).

Paul uses three terms to describe this gift of grace that God offers us in Christ. First, we are "justified," that is, God gives us the verdict of acquittal, declaring us forgiven of any wrongdoing. Second, God gives us "redemption," that is, he frees us from our captivity, buying us back from the condition of slavery. Third, God creates "atonement," or expiation of sin, through the sacrifice of Christ on the cross (v. 25).

In all of this, God shows his faithfulness to humanity and his deep desire to bring rebellious humanity back to himself. Since there is only one God for all people, God will justify all people in the same way—Jew and Gentile, circumcised and uncircumcised (vv. 29–30). Whatever our background or accomplishments, whether we are part of God's chosen ones or not, we are saved only by God's grace. Because of Christ, there is no longer any reason to boast. We cannot prove our worth before God by what we complete or achieve. Through Christ on the cross, we are delivered from all our attempts to make ourselves acceptable to God by the things we do. We can only hope for salvation through the grace manifested in Jesus Christ and accepted by faith.

After grappling with Paul's teachings, test your understanding by answering these questions:

‡ How would I describe what God has done for us in Christ without using Paul's theological language?

‡ Why is God's process for justifying sinners the same for both Jews and Gentiles?

Meditatio

Read again the passages that seem most pertinent to you. Ask yourself what they mean in the context of your own life experiences.

‡ Faith is my own acceptance of what God has done for me in Christ, a response that implies a faithful relationship with Christ. How have I experienced the growth of faith in my life? How do I want my faith to develop more?

‡ No action on my part could ever earn or deserve what God has done for me in Christ. All I have, even my faith, is a result of God's gift of grace. How does this reflection deepen my understanding of my life in relationship to God?

‡ Paul implies that placing our trust in the lordship of Christ creates a radical reorientation of our attitude toward ourselves and our fellow human beings. How has my life been reoriented through my growing faith in Christ as Lord?

Oratio

Speak to God in response to the teachings of Paul. Pray to the One who knows you intimately, cares about you deeply, and accepts you unconditionally.

> Father of our Lord Jesus Christ, you have forgiven me of sin and redeemed me from death through the cross of your only Son. Help me respond to your grace with trusting confidence and with deepening dedication to your plan for my life.

Continue speaking to God in whatever ways seem to respond to the divine Word spoken to you . . .

Contemplatio

The wonders of God's grace remind us that nothing we can do will ever merit or deserve our life in Christ. Imaginatively place yourself in the hands of our compassionate God and know that love is God's gift without conditions.

Write a few words about your contemplative experience.

Operatio

What is my motivation for the work that I do, if not to earn God's favor and blessings? What would be different about my life if I truly believed that all is grace?

27

Transformed by the Love of God

Listen to Paul's teachings about how God has taken the initiative in our lives and transformed us in the process. Consider the effects of Paul's words on his ancient audience in Rome as his letter was read at their Sunday worship.

ROMANS 5:1–11

¹Therefore, since we are justified by faith, we have peace with God through our Lord Jesus Christ, ²through whom we have obtained access to this grace in which we stand; and we boast in our hope of sharing the glory of God. ³And not only that, but we also boast in our sufferings, knowing that suffering produces endurance, ⁴and endurance produces character, and character produces hope, ⁵and hope does not disappoint us, because God's love has been poured into our hearts through the Holy Spirit that has been given to us.

⁶For while we were still weak, at the right time Christ died for the ungodly. ⁷Indeed, rarely will anyone die for a righteous person—though perhaps for a good person someone might actually dare to die. ⁸But God proves his love for us in that while we still were sinners Christ died for us. ⁹Much more surely then, now that we have been

justified by his blood, will we be saved through him from the wrath of God. [10]For if while we were enemies, we were reconciled to God through the death of his Son, much more surely, having been reconciled, will we be saved by his life. [11]But more than that, we even boast in God through our Lord Jesus Christ, through whom we have now received reconciliation.

Resurrection

After receiving Paul's words into your heart, continue searching for the meaning and significance of his words to the Romans and to the world.

In this jubilant text, Paul summarizes the divine process that leads to our salvation. He urges us to look to the future with confidence, ironically using the term "boasting" throughout the passage. Previously Paul had described "boasting" negatively, as a prideful confidence that rested on our own achievement or privileged status (3:27). But now Paul proposes a boasting that is certainly legitimate because it rests solely on the work God has done on our behalf.

When we accept the redeeming death of Christ through our response in faith, we are "justified" (v. 1) and "reconciled" (v. 10) to God. Both words refer to the restoration of our relationship with God that had been lost through sin. We now have access to God's grace and are able to stand firmly and confidently within this grace (v. 2). As a result of Christ's death for us and our acceptance of God's grace through faith, we have "peace" and "hope." Peace is the foretaste of the fullness of salvation that we await. Hope is the confident expectation that we will share fully in the glory of God.

God's grace within us is strong enough to give us peace and hope even in the midst of adversity (vv. 3–4). Paul knows from his own experience that God's grace enables our sufferings to deepen our hope and lead us to God. Of course, suffering does not necessarily produce "endurance," and endurance doesn't always result in "character." Adversity often produces resentment and bitterness. But endurance, character, and hope are qualities of grace, and they develop when the believer stands justified before God and responds to adversity in faith.

The whole process of God's action on our behalf is rooted in God's love for us. In a way unparalleled by human love, God has given himself to us without restraint: "God's love has been poured into our hearts" (v. 5). The image is that of life-giving water being poured on a thirsty land, torrential rains in an arid desert. God's love gushes forth into our hearts with abandon by the Holy Spirit.

It is impossible for us to understand the dimensions of divine love, but we can see the manifestation of God's love in the death of his Son for us: "God proves his love for us in that while we still were sinners Christ died for us" (v. 8). God's love (*agape* in Greek) is unconditional love, independent of any worthiness or merit on our part. God's act of love is humanly inconceivable and contrary to all expectations (v. 7), demonstrating beyond doubt God's personal love for us.

Paul's encouraging text is oriented toward the future when we will be "saved" through Christ (vv. 9–10). The peace and the hope we experience in the present is just a taste of the fullness of salvation yet to come. We know in our hearts through hope that we will experience the salvation that has been promised us by God. The process of salvation will be complete when we share "the glory of God" (v. 2), the full image and likeness of God, as our Creator intends. In faith we trust God completely to finish the work of our salvation and bring us to the glory he has promised.

After seeking to understand the implications of Paul's teaching about our transformation in God's love, answer these questions:

‡ What are the words that describe our former life (vv. 6, 8, 10)?

‡ How does God "prove" (v. 8) his love for us? Why is this proof so convincing?

Meditatio

Ask yourself how God is speaking to you in this passage and how you can respond with trust and confidence.

‡ How has adversity affected my own life? In what ways have I experienced suffering that led to endurance, character, and hope?

‡ How would I describe the peace and hope that I experience as a result of God's grace at work within me?

‡ For what reasons does Paul say we can be confident in God's plans for us? Is confidence in the future a characteristic of my life? How could I deepen my confidence?

Oratio

Pray with trust and confidence in whatever way God gives to you as a result of his grace.

> Lord Jesus Christ, you died for us while we were still sinners as the clear proof of God's unconditional love. Help me to open my heart through faith so that the Holy Spirit may fill it with divine love, and give me confidence in the glory of God to come.

Continue to pray in response to the Word you have heard . . .

Contemplatio

Draw up as much hope, trust, and confidence as you can from God's promises and rest in that blessed assurance.

Write a few words that linger from your silent time in God's presence.

Operatio

What new hope and confidence have I received from my lectio divina? How can my life be characterized by more trust and confidence in God?

28

Dying and Rising with Christ in Baptism

Lectio

Listen to what Paul taught the early Christians about the meaning of their baptism. Read these words aloud, as they were pronounced during Christian baptisms in ancient Rome.

ROMANS 6:3–14

³Do you not know that all of us who have been baptized into Christ Jesus were baptized into his death? ⁴Therefore we have been buried with him by baptism into death, so that, just as Christ was raised from the dead by the glory of the Father, so we too might walk in newness of life.

⁵For if we have been united with him in a death like his, we will certainly be united with him in a resurrection like his. ⁶We know that our old self was crucified with him so that the body of sin might be destroyed, and we might no longer be enslaved to sin. ⁷For whoever has died is freed from sin. ⁸But if we have died with Christ, we believe that we will also live with him. ⁹We know that Christ, being raised from the dead, will never die again; death no longer has dominion over him. ¹⁰The death he died, he died to sin, once for all; but the life he lives, he lives to God. ¹¹So you also must consider yourselves dead to sin and alive to God in Christ Jesus.

¹²Therefore, do not let sin exercise dominion in your mortal bodies, to make you obey their passions. ¹³No longer present your members to sin as instruments of wickedness, but present yourselves to God as those who have been brought from death to life, and present your members to God as instruments of righteousness. ¹⁴For sin will have no dominion over you, since you are not under law but under grace.

Having listened carefully to Paul's words, continue exploring the meaning of his words to the community in Rome.

Paul assumes that the Roman Christians have a general understanding of baptism, the sacramental action that joins a believer to Christ. Through the tradition they had received from the earliest disciples, they know that when a person is "baptized into Christ Jesus" a very real change occurs. The believer's being is transformed and intimately united with Christ and his destiny so that what is true of Christ becomes true of the one baptized.

The baptisteries of churches through the ages have been metaphorically compared to a tomb and a womb, because through baptism a believer dies with Christ and is born anew. The believer descends into the baptismal pool, is covered with its waters, and emerges into a new life. Faith and baptism, Paul teaches, are the real beginning of a new life. Through accepting in faith the grace of God in Christ, we are justified. Through our baptism into Christ, we begin the process of being sanctified. The dying and rising of Christ, the means of our justification, become the pattern of our sanctification. While we are truly "in Christ" by baptism, our lives are a step-by-step movement into Christlikeness. The new life of a baptized Christian is a life of continually being united to the dying and rising of Christ.

The death that the believer undergoes in baptism is a real dying with Christ. Paul says that we are "baptized into his death" (v. 3). This includes our entry into Christ's tomb: "buried with him by baptism into death" (v. 4). Since by dying on the cross Christ defeated sin, in our dying with Christ the power of sin no longer controls our lives. "Our old self was crucified" with Christ; therefore the dominating influence of sin has been destroyed and we are no longer enslaved to it (v. 6).

But that is only half of our baptism. In dying, Christ conquered sin; in rising, he conquered death. As Christ was raised from the dead, we too have the vitality of eternal life within us, so "we too might walk in newness of life" (v. 4). This living in life's newness flows from the resurrection of Jesus and belongs essentially to the age to come, but it is a reality that begins now as a prelude to our future resurrection. By living in union with Christ, we walk in the age to come.

Finally, Paul turns from theological explanation to moral exhortation, from descriptive to imperative (vv. 12–14). He moves from what God has done for us in faith and baptism to what God wants from us in the Christian life, from the fact of justification to the ongoing challenge of sanctification. Freed from sin's enslaving dominion over us, we can now present our lives before another master. No longer must we offer our bodies to the tyranny of sin as "instruments of wickedness." We can now offer our bodies, with all their members, talents, and abilities, to the reign of God as "instruments of righteousness" (v. 13).

Our life in Christ today is an existence with one foot in the old life and one in the new. We live in the tension between sin and grace, flesh and spirit, death and life. Our fallen human nature pulls in one direction, while our reborn life in Christ pulls even more powerfully in the other. We are already living in the risen Christ, and our freedom from sin and death is evident in the orientation of our lives. Yet, the complete realization of our resurrection awaits the future, when the whole significance of Christ's dying and rising and of our baptism into him will become fully manifest.

After hearing Paul's teaching to the Romans, try to answer these questions about the text:

☩ In what way are we freed from sin by dying with Christ?

☩ Why is a baptistery referred to as both a tomb and a womb?

Meditatio

Repeat and ponder whatever words strike you most from your lectio. Reflect on how God is deepening your understanding and enriching your hope for the future.

‡ What aspect of my baptism have I forgotten or neglected? What is Paul teaching me anew in this passage?

‡ Through baptism, I can "walk in newness of life." How do I know that the purpose of Christian faith is not about life after death? What indicates to me that I am living my future resurrection already in the present?

‡ As one who is reborn in Christ, how do I experience the pull between sin and grace, the old life and the new? What gives me assurance that my life is destined for the life of resurrection?

Oratio

Having listened and reflected on God's Word to you in the text, now respond to God from your heart in prayer.

Crucified and risen Lord, in baptism my old self was crucified and buried with you in the tomb. Renew the grace of baptism within me so that sin has no power in my life and I may walk in newness of life.

Continue praying in whatever words seem to express the content of your heart...

Contemplatio

Believe in the transforming power of your baptism. In silent confidence, know that God's Spirit is continuing to transform you into the likeness of Christ.

What words come to mind after your contemplative time in God's presence?

Operatio

What can I do to stir up the power of baptism in my life? What difference does it make to know that I am walking in newness of life?

29

Confidence in
God's Love Made Known
in Christ Jesus

Lectio

Read aloud Paul's jubilant praise of God's love addressed to the church in Rome. Allow the assurance of God's unfathomable love to lift you up.

ROMANS 8:28–39

28We know that all things work together for good for those who love God, who are called according to his purpose. 29For those whom he foreknew he also predestined to be conformed to the image of his Son, in order that he might be the firstborn within a large family. 30And those whom he predestined he also called; and those whom he called he also justified; and those whom he justified he also glorified.

31What then are we to say about these things? If God is for us, who is against us? 32He who did not withhold his own Son, but gave him up for all of us, will he not with him also give us everything else? 33Who will bring any charge against God's elect? It is God who justifies. 34Who is to condemn? It is Christ Jesus, who died, yes, who was raised, who is at the right hand of God, who indeed intercedes for us. 35Who will separate us from the love of Christ? Will hardship, or

distress, or persecution, or famine, or nakedness, or peril, or sword?
[36]As it is written,

> "For your sake we are being killed all day long;
> we are accounted as sheep to be slaughtered."

[37]No, in all these things we are more than conquerors through him who loved us. [38]For I am convinced that neither death, nor life, nor angels, nor rulers, nor things present, nor things to come, nor powers, [39]nor height, nor depth, nor anything else in all creation, will be able to separate us from the love of God in Christ Jesus our Lord.

With new hope experienced through God's Word, continue listening for the full significance of Paul's text.

The love of God, made visible in what Jesus has done for humanity, is the foundation of Christian life and hope. We can have absolute confidence in our future because we know it is in the hands of our all-powerful and all-loving God, not our own. Paul assures us that "all things work together for good" for those whose lives are enveloped in God's love (v. 28). God even uses our worst suffering for good purposes, for the sake of our salvation, the full realization of God's eternal plan for us. Our destiny is firmly set in God's purposes: to transform us into the glorified image of Christ and to bring us into the family of God forever (vv. 29–30). Absolutely nothing can disturb that unshakable hope. In the remainder of this jubilant passage, Paul sings of the victory that God has gained for humanity over all the powers that might conceivably oppose that love.

"God is for us" (v. 31)—this is the essence of the gospel Paul proclaims. As with all great truths, its articulation is disarmingly simple. With elevated eloquence, Paul praises God for his absolute faithfulness verified for the world in the person of Jesus Christ, "who died, . . . who was raised, who is at the right hand of God, who indeed intercedes for us" (v. 34). As the one who died, Jesus redeemed humanity from sin and judgment; as the one who was raised, he assures us of victory over death and the gift of eternal life. As the one at the right hand of God, Jesus reigns as Lord in power and glory. As the one who intercedes for us, the enthroned Lord exercises his authority on our behalf. Jesus assures us that God is for us, not only in his sacrificial love on the cross but also now in his sustaining love as our glorious Lord.

The faithfulness of God's love is extolled through six rhetorical questions (vv. 31-35). The questions answer themselves and praise the God who is always with us. With God on our side, the forces that are marshaled against us cannot prevail. Since God even gave up his Son for our sake, paying the highest possible price, we can certainly trust God to give us everything we could possibly need (v. 32). Because the only one of any significance who could bring a charge against us or condemn us is the one who has done everything for us, then truly we have nothing to be afraid of (vv. 33–34). Since God has proven his love for us absolutely, we need not worry about any opposition.

Not even the greatest dangers and most painful experiences that humans could undergo can separate us from God's love (vv. 35–36). Since God has made us "more than conquerors" (v. 37), having conquered the greatest of all enemies through Christ, we can live with absolute confidence that God is for us. Not even the strongest forces of the universe—earthly or cosmic, natural or supernatural, present or future—can separate us from God's love (vv. 38–39). Paul uses all the fiercest terms he can imagine to show how ineradicable is the divine love that he has come to know through Jesus Christ.

Having listened to Paul's confident praise of God's love, think about these questions:

‡ What is the essence of God's eternal plan for us?

‡ How does Paul assure us that we have absolutely nothing to fear?

Meditatio

Spend some time meditating on the words of the text you have read. Let God's Word touch your heart deeply and work to bring confidence to your spirit.

‡ What distinguishes confident hope from wishful thinking? How does this passage help make my Christian hope convinced and certain?

‡ In what way is "God is for us" the gospel of Paul in a nutshell? How have I experienced the practical implications of these words?

‡ Which of the threats mentioned in verses 35 and 38 are most real to me? Why can they not separate me from God's love?

have gifts that differ according to the grace given to us: prophecy, in proportion to faith; [7]ministry, in ministering; the teacher, in teaching; [8]the exhorter, in exhortation; the giver, in generosity; the leader, in diligence; the compassionate, in cheerfulness.

[9]Let love be genuine; hate what is evil, hold fast to what is good; [10]love one another with mutual affection; outdo one another in showing honor. [11]Do not lag in zeal, be ardent in spirit, serve the Lord. [12]Rejoice in hope, be patient in suffering, persevere in prayer. [13]Contribute to the needs of the saints; extend hospitality to strangers.

[14]Bless those who persecute you; bless and do not curse them. [15]Rejoice with those who rejoice, weep with those who weep. [16]Live in harmony with one another; do not be haughty, but associate with the lowly; do not claim to be wiser than you are. [17]Do not repay anyone evil for evil, but take thought for what is noble in the sight of all. [18]If it is possible, so far as it depends on you, live peaceably with all. [19]Beloved, never avenge yourselves, but leave room for the wrath of God; for it is written, "Vengeance is mine, I will repay, says the Lord." [20]No, "if your enemies are hungry, feed them; if they are thirsty, give them something to drink; for by doing this you will heap burning coals on their heads." [21]Do not be overcome by evil, but overcome evil with good.

Continue exploring Paul's encouraging words through the understanding of the faith community.

Paul concludes his letter to the Romans by summoning the community to a pattern of living in response to the gospel they have received. The grace we have been given in Christ is not an abstraction but a gift that gives shape and direction for Christian living. Paul exhorts the community to present their bodies as "a living sacrifice, holy and acceptable to God" (v. 1). Like the temple sacrifices given to God in worship, Christians are urged to offer their whole lives as a holy offering in worship of God.

In order to live the Christian life as a sacrificial consecration to God, Paul insists that his readers not be "conformed" to the world with all its superficial and passing attractions but be "transformed" by the power of grace to live in a new way of life (v. 2). God's transforming grace renews our minds, giving us the power to discern what is necessary to live according to "the will of God" in the often difficult and confusing situations we face in the world. The obedience of life flowing from that discernment makes of our lives a continual and "living sacrifice" that is acceptable and pleasing to God.

Paul then begins to offer more detailed guidance for relationships within the Christian community (vv. 3–8). Considering that faith and the spiritual gifts are a result of God's grace, believers must judge themselves and their gifts humbly in relationship to the community. The metaphor of the body expresses the ideal of a diversity of gifts within a unity of faith. As "one body in Christ," the church is made up of many members who have no need to compete with one another but who freely complement one another for the sake of the whole. Each member is given "gifts that differ according to the grace given to us" (v. 6). Offering a representative sample of these gifts and their functions, Paul emphasizes that they are not the possessions of the members but are endowments to be used for ministry within the community.

Paul's remaining exhortations offer a description of the Christian life as a holy and living sacrifice to God. Love heads the list and penetrates the entire sequence. Paul first describes love within the Christian community (vv. 9–13) and then love within the wider society (vv. 14–21). Christian love is not shaped by the natural inclinations of our fallen nature nor by the standards of the world but by the power of God's Spirit transforming the mind and will of believers according to the standards of the new age in Christ.

Paul's advice on the love of Christians within the church is modeled on the affectionate love within families, the generous love of spouses and the patient care of siblings for one another. His counsel for Christian love within the wider world, however, offers a practical application of Jesus's command to love one's enemies (Matt. 5:44) and a call for nonretaliation in the face of opposition and persecution. Though God's will for us who believe is significantly different from our instinctive response, God is transforming us in the Spirit to receive, understand, and obey his radical teachings for life in the world. To bless our persecutors and not avenge our wrongs require the selflessness that only the power of God's love can bestow. The converted heart is able to discern God's will, to know what is "good and acceptable and perfect" (v. 2), and to "overcome evil with good" (v. 21) through union with the resurrected Lord and the power of his Spirit within.

Meditatio

Reflect on your own life as a living sacrifice to God. Consider how this vision of your life's purpose offers focus and meaning to the things you do.

‡ Part of Christian responsibility is to discover one's unique gift and then use it for the glory of God within the church. Which of the gifts listed in verses 6–8 is most like my gift? How can I put this to greater use for the good of others?

‡ What does Paul mean when he says, "Let love be genuine" (v. 9)? How can I tell when my love is "genuine" and when it is "conformed to this world" (v. 2)?

‡ What do I admire most about Paul after studying his life and teachings?

Oratio

Respond to Paul's teachings with prayer to God. Ask for the gifts you need to make your life a holy and living sacrifice to God.

> God of divine mercy, you have given me the gift of your Spirit to renew my mind and convert my heart so that I can discern your will. Give me the humility to see my life in Christ as your gift and to love genuinely as Christ has loved me.

Continue to express a prayer of gratitude from your heart...

Contemplatio

Contemplate your life as a living sacrifice to God. Spend some silent time asking God to give you the experience of humble gratitude for your life in Christ.

Write a few words to conclude your time of peaceful contemplation.

Operatio

Paul gives many examples of love in both personal relationships and the wider society. What can I do to put into practice the radical demands of Christian love in my family, school, work, and church?

Ancient-Future Bible
Study for Small Groups

A small group for *collatio*, the communal practice of lectio divina, is a wonderful way to let the power of Scripture more deeply nourish participants. Through the thoughts, reflections, prayers, and experiences of the other members of the group, each individual comes to understand Scripture more intensely and experience it more profoundly. By sharing our understanding and wisdom in a faith-filled group of people, we discover how to let God live in every dimension of our lives and we enrich the lives of others.

These groups may be formed in any number of ways, just as you create groups for other learning experiences within your community. Groups composed of no more than a dozen people are best for this experience. It is preferable to give people with various needs a variety of days and times from which to choose.

Small groups are best formed when people are encouraged and supported by a church's pastoral leadership and personally welcomed into these small communities. Personally directed invitations are most effective for convincing people to add another dimension to their schedules.

The collatio should never take the place of one's regular, personal lectio divina. Rather, a weekly communal practice is an ideal extension and continuation of personal, daily sacred reading. At each group session, participants discuss the fruits of their individual lectio divina and practice elements of lectio divina together.

Participants should read carefully the opening sections of this book before joining the group. "The Movements of Lectio Divina," "The Essence of Lectio Divina," and "Your Personal Practice of Ancient-Future

Bible Study" would be helpful sections to review throughout the course of the study.

The full weekly collatio group session is designed for about ninety minutes. Those groups with limited time may choose either Part 1 or Part 2 for the group experience. Instructions for each of the collatio groups are provided on the following pages.

Suggestions for Participating in the Group

✝ The spirit of the collatio should be that of a personal conversation, with the members desiring to learn from one another and building each other up. The divine Word is the teacher; the members of the group are all learners.

✝ When participating in the group, members should offer their thoughts, insights, and feelings about the sacred text. The group can avoid the distraction of off-topic chatter by sticking to the text, the commentary, and their personal response to the text from the meditatio.

✝ Group members should be careful to give everyone in the group an opportunity to share. When discussing personal thoughts, members should use "I" language and be cautious about giving advice to others. They should listen attentively to the other members of the group so as to learn from their insights and should not worry about trying to cover all the questions in each gathering. They should select only those that seem the most helpful for group discussion.

✝ Dispute, debate, and dogmatic hairsplitting within the group erode its focus and purpose. Opposition and division destroy the supportive bond of the group. The desire of individuals to assert themselves and their own ideas wears down the spirit of the group. In a community setting, it is often wise to "agree to disagree." An inflexible, pedantic attitude blocks the way to a vital and fulfilling understanding of the passage. The Scriptures are the living Word of God, the full meaning of which we can never exhaust.

✝ It is usually helpful to have someone to guide the process of the group. This facilitator directs the discussion, helping the group keep the discussion on time and on track. The facilitator need not be an expert, either in Scripture or in the process of lectio divina, but simply a person with the skills necessary to guide a group. This role may be rotated among members of the group, if desired.

Group Study in Six Sessions

‡ Begin each group session with hospitality and welcome. Name tags are helpful if group members don't know one another. Offer any announcements or instructions before entering the spirit of prayer.

‡ Set the tone and focus the group by saying the gathering prayer together.

‡ Note that the first group session is a bit different from the others because it involves reading and discussing the introduction. After the first group session, all the remaining sessions follow the same format.

‡ The group sessions are in two parts. Part 1 is a discussion of the fruits of the lectio divina that participants completed on their own since the last group session. The most effective question to ask of each chapter is this: "What is your most important insight from this chapter?" Group members may mention insights they gained in the lectio, meditatio, oratio, contemplatio, or operatio of each chapter.

‡ Part 2 is a session of lectio divina in the group. Leave at least half of the group time for this section. Move through each of the five movements as described in the chapter. Read the text aloud, followed by the commentary. Leave the most time for the more personal questions of the meditatio. Don't worry if you don't complete them all.

‡ Leave sufficient time for the oratio, contemplatio, and operatio. These movements should not be rushed. Gently guide the group from vocal prayer into a period of restful silence. Don't neglect to conclude the lectio divina by mentioning some practical fruits of operatio before dismissing the group into the world of daily discipleship.

‡ Conclude each group session by encouraging participants to complete the lectio divina on their own for the upcoming chapters. Ask them to write their responses to each movement of lectio in their book.

Collatio Group 1

‡ The first group session is a bit different from the others. After offering greetings and introductions, explain the process of Ancient-Future Bible Study. Then set the tone for the group experience by praying together the gathering prayer.

‡ Gathering prayer:

> Come upon us, Holy Spirit, to enlighten and guide us as we begin this study of Paul, apostle to the nations. You have inspired Paul and the authors of Scripture to write a Word that has the power to convert our hearts and change our lives. Give us a sense of expectation, and help us to trust that you will shine the light of your truth within us. Bless us as we gather with your gifts of wisdom and discernment so that we may listen to the inspired Word and experience its transforming energy.

‡ Spend the first half of the collatio group reading the introduction to this book and discussing the questions to consider. A volunteer may read each section aloud, and the group will spend a few minutes discussing the questions that follow.

‡ Spend the second half of the group time following the five movements of the lectio divina at the end of the introduction. Read the text aloud, followed by the commentary. Then spend time reflecting and sharing responses to the questions of the meditatio.

‡ When leading into the oratio, pray the prayer aloud, then leave time for additional prayers from the group. When the vocal prayer has receded, lead the group into contemplatio. Help the group to feel comfortable with the quiet and to relax in the presence of God. Conclude the lectio divina with the operatio. Share encouragement and commitment to practice lectio divina throughout the week.

‡ Before departing, instruct group members in their practice of lectio divina during the week. Participants should complete the lectio divina for chapters 1–5 for next week. Encourage them to write their responses to each movement of lectio in their book. The lectio divina for chapter 6 will be done together in the group next week.

Collatio Group 2

✝ Gathering prayer:

> *Creating and redeeming God, you blessed Saul of Tarsus with a revelation of the risen Christ and called him to be your apostle. For the sake of the gospel, he crossed the boundaries that divided peoples from one another. Widen our vision and deepen our understanding so that, like Paul, we may become "all things to all people" for the sake of Christ. Throughout these moments together, continue to transform our hearts and give us a passionate desire for your Word.*

✝ Part 1:
- Having completed the lectio divina for chapters 1–5 during the week, the group members discuss the fruit of their practice for these five chapters. Divide the chapters into equal time allotments so that no chapter is neglected. To provoke personal discussion of each chapter, ask this question: "What insight is most significant to you from your reflection on this chapter?"

✝ Part 2:
- Spend at least the last half of the group time in the full lectio divina of chapter 6. Move through each step according to the instructions provided in the chapter, leaving plenty of time for oratio, contemplatio, and operatio.

✝ Departure:
- Encourage participants to complete the lectio divina for chapters 7–11 before the next collatio group. Ask them to write their responses to each movement of lectio in their book. The lectio divina for chapter 12 will be done together in the group next week.

Collatio Group 3

✝ Gathering prayer:

> *God of all people, you are the God in whom we live and move and have our being. As Paul used the faith of Jerusalem and the reason of Athens for the spread of the gospel, help us engage our minds and receive your grace as we study your inspired Word. The hearts of all people are restless and searching for you. Give us a deep desire to understand, accept, and live your Word as disciples of Jesus your Son.*

✝ Part 1:
  • Having completed the lectio divina for chapters 7–11 during the week, the group members discuss the fruit of their practice for these five chapters. Divide the chapters into equal time allotments so that no chapter is neglected. To provoke personal discussion of each chapter, ask this question: "What insight is most significant to you from your reflection on this chapter?"

✝ Part 2:
  • Spend at least the last half of the group time in the full lectio divina of chapter 12. Move through each step according to the instructions provided in the chapter, leaving plenty of time for oratio, contemplatio, and operatio.

✝ Departure:
  • Encourage participants to complete the lectio divina for chapters 13–17 before the next collatio group. Ask them to write their responses to each movement of lectio in their book. The lectio divina for chapter 18 will be done together in the group next week.

Collatio Group 4

> *Abba, our Father, you have chosen us as your people and*
> *called us to the life of salvation in Christ. We are grateful for*
> *this community of faith in which we are gathered and for all*
> *those who help us understand your Word and live in Christ.*
> *Continue challenging us to be boundary breakers, to eliminate*
> *the divisions that divide people from one another and create a*
> *higher unity in Christ. Relieve our fears and anxieties, and help*
> *us live as people of confidence and hope.*

♱ Part 1:

- Having completed the lectio divina for chapters 13–17 during the week, the group members discuss the fruit of their practice for these five chapters. Divide the chapters into equal time allotments so that no chapter is neglected. To provoke personal discussion of each chapter, ask this question: "What insight is most significant to you from your reflection on this chapter?"

♱ Part 2:

- Spend at least the last half of the group time in the full lectio divina of chapter 18. Move through each step according to the instructions provided in the chapter, leaving plenty of time for oratio, contemplatio, and operatio.

♱ Departure:

- Encourage participants to complete the lectio divina for chapters 19–23 before the next collatio group. Ask them to write their responses to each movement of lectio in their book. The lectio divina for chapter 24 will be done together in the group next week.

Collatio Group 5

✝ Gathering prayer:

> *Lord our God, we proclaim Christ crucified and risen in imitation of your apostle Paul. He experienced the dying of Jesus in the suffering of his own body so that we might experience the life of Jesus within us. Help us to reverently bear the light and treasure of the gospel within the fragile vessels of our own lives so that others may experience the life we have come to know in Christ. Keep us faithful to the gospel so that your power and wisdom may be known in our world today.*

✝ Part 1:
- Having completed the lectio divina for chapters 19–23 during the week, the group members discuss the fruit of their practice for these five chapters. Divide the chapters into equal time allotments so that no chapter is neglected. To provoke personal discussion of each chapter, ask this question: "What insight is most significant to you from your reflection on this chapter?"

✝ Part 2:
- Spend at least the last half of the group time in the full lectio divina of chapter 24. Move through each step according to the instructions provided in the chapter, leaving plenty of time for oratio, contemplatio, and operatio.

✝ Departure:
- Encourage participants to complete the lectio divina for chapters 25–29 before the next collatio group. Ask them to write their responses to each movement of lectio in their book. The lectio divina for chapter 30 will be done together in the group next week.

Collatio Group 6

✟ Gathering prayer:

> *Merciful God, you have proven your unconditional love for us by forgiving our sin and redeeming us from death through the saving cross of Jesus your Son. As you continue to pour your love into our hearts, let us experience the power of your Holy Spirit within us. Help us to open our lives to the grace of our baptism so that we may always walk in genuine freedom and live in newness of life. Bless us as we gather in the name of Jesus, and make us witnesses of his life in our world.*

✟ Part 1:
- Having completed the lectio divina for chapters 25–29 during the week, the group members discuss the fruit of their practice for these five chapters. Divide the chapters into equal time allotments so that no chapter is neglected. To provoke personal discussion of each chapter, ask this question: "What insight is most significant to you from your reflection on this chapter?"

✟ Part 2:
- Spend at least the last half of the group time in the full lectio divina of chapter 30. Move through each step according to the instructions provided in the chapter, leaving plenty of time for oratio, contemplatio, and operatio.

✟ Departure:
- Discuss how this Ancient-Future Bible Study has made a difference in the lives of group members and whether the group wishes to study another book in the series. Consult www.brazospress.com/ancient futurebiblestudy for more study options.